Date Due

NOV 1 5 1980			
APR 1 5 1981			
MAY 1 5 1981			
2002			
12-15-95			
DEC 2 0 1995			

BRODART, INC. Cat. No. 23 233 Printed in U.S.A.

Crinolines and Crimping Irons

Crinolines and Crimping Irons

VICTORIAN CLOTHES:
HOW THEY WERE CLEANED AND CARED FOR

Christina Walkley and Vanda Foster

PETER OWEN · LONDON

ISBN 0 7206 0500 8

To Anne Buck, author of *Victorian Costume
and Costume Accessories,* and first Keeper
of The Gallery of English Costume, Manchester.

PETER OWEN LIMITED
73 Kenway Road London SW5 0RE

First British Commonwealth edition 1978
© Vanda Foster and Christina Walkley 1978

Printed in Great Britain by
Daedalus Press Crown House Stoke Ferry King's Lynn

CONTENTS

PLATES

The plates are reproduced by kind permission of The Gallery of English Costume, City of Manchester Art Galleries. The material in Appendix 3 and the line illustrations on pp. 55, 88, 118, 134 and 136 are reproduced from *Harrod's Catalogue* of 1895 by kind permission of Messrs Harrods Ltd and Messrs David & Charles Ltd.

INTRODUCTION

The question 'How did the Victorian woman clean her clothes?' is too often answered either by 'She gave them to her servants to clean,' or by 'She didn't.' The first answer is only partially correct – the average Victorian housewife was far more actively involved in the running of her home than is generally recognized – and in any case merely invites the further question, 'How did the servants manage?' The second is grossly unjust to the age which above all others placed cleanliness next to godliness. The truth is that the Victorian woman maintained the most scrupulous standards of clothes care, and expended an energy and patience in pursuit of her aim which seem astounding to her great-granddaughters.

The task was not an easy one. Far greater numbers of clothes were worn then, and the average household was considerably larger than a modern one. Despite the high rate of infant mortality, to have upwards of six children was the norm. Birth control began to be practised in the 1870s, but was at first restricted to the upper classes. The lower middle class, who set a high premium on material advancement, were perhaps the next to follow suit: thus in *Lark Rise to Candleford,* Flora Thompson's evocative trilogy of novels describing her childhood in a country village in the 1880s, Mr and Mrs Green surprise Laura by announcing that they do not intend to have more than one child. 'Not *intend* to have more! What say would they have in the matter?' wonders Laura, and her surprise is not only due to her youth, for her fellow-villagers continued to produce huge families until the end of the century, and it was a long time before there was any significant drop in the birth rate.

Besides the large numbers of children, the household was often extended by grandparents or other relatives, to say nothing of the servants who, although they were there to lessen the work-load, could not help contributing to it as well. In 1879, *Sylvia's Home Journal* assumed an average household to consist of eight people – master and mistress, two children, cook, housemaid, nurse and laundrymaid. This is an unusually high servant-to-family ratio, and a surprisingly small number of children, but it illustrates how easily the Victorian household could reach exactly twice the size of a comparable modern one.

To have servants was not necessarily a sign of wealth, and even less one of leisure: more often it meant that there was simply too much work for one person to get through unaided. This situation is easy to visualize if we imagine our own lives stripped of domestic appliances, easy-care fabrics and convenience foods. Furthermore labour was cheap. The very rich, of course, entrusted the total care of their households to domestics, under the overall supervision of a capable and well-paid housekeeper; when the merely lazy or incompetent tried to emulate them the results were disastrous, as Dickens's Dora Copperfield shows. By far the most common procedure was for the mistress herself to act as housekeeper, personally undertaking the more sophisticated tasks such as washing the best china or 'getting up' her lace, and directing and supervising her staff in the other jobs. In the words of Mrs Beeton, 'As with the commander of an army or the leader of any enterprise, so it is with the mistress of a house.' Indeed in the humbler households the mistress had perforce to participate in every aspect of the housework, using her maid only as an extra pair of hands. Thus in Mrs Gaskell's *Cranford,* set at the very beginning of our period, 'when Mrs Forrester, for instance, gave a party in her baby-house of a dwelling, and the little maiden disturbed the ladies on the sofa by a request that she might get the tea-tray out from underneath, every one took this novel proceeding as the most natural thing in the world, and talked on about household forms and ceremonies as if we all believed that our hostess had a regular servants' hall, second table, with housekeeper and steward, instead of the one little charity-school maiden, whose short ruddy arms could never have been strong enough to carry the tray upstairs, if she had not been assisted in private by her mistress, who now sat in state, pretending not to know what cakes were sent up, though she knew, and we knew, and she knew that we knew, and we knew that she knew that we knew, she had been busy all the morning making teabread and sponge-cakes.' Most of Flora Thompson's contemporaries from Lark Rise started their working lives at the age of eleven or twelve in a post of this sort, helping their employer much as a daughter might, in exchange for living as one of the family and receiving a tiny wage, and most of them fared very well.

Although a large number of households employed help of some

kind throughout the period, circumstances did change, and by the last two decades of the century we read everywhere of a serious shortage of servants. This affected all but the very rich, and many a woman found herself having to undertake a greater proportion of the family housework than ever before. Various factors in society had led to this shortage of servants. In urban areas factory work had always presented a tempting alternative to those who loved their freedom, but the improved education brought about by the Education Act of 1870 and its successors opened up new fields even to rural girls. Thus Flora Thompson's Laura was able to enter the Post Office as a clerk, where for her mother there had been no alternative to service. Although bitter complaints were voiced against women snatching away men's jobs, an indubitable factor in the increased scope of female employment was the acute short-age of men. The Crimean War and the upkeep – both military and administrative – of the Empire, took their toll in men's lives, and by the last quarter of the nineteenth century there was a surplus of a million women. As marriage could no longer be considered a viable career, some kind of employment had to be found for these women; fortunately for them the boom in industry and trade had brought in its wake a whole crop of new jobs in shops and offices, which in turn broadened the horizons of the working girl.

Maintenance of the family clothes and linen was a mammoth task. Very little mechanical help was available. The man who announced in 1876 that 'the various household implements and machines which men have gradually invented to lighten labour having now become the real hewers of wood and drawers of water for the women of this century, there is scarcely any severe or tedious drudgery to perform,'[1] had clearly never experienced a wash-day at first hand. Although washing machines had been introduced at the very beginning of the century, they were hardly labour-saving since the rotating motion had to be activated by hand. Wringers appeared some time later, and certainly made life easier, but ironing was still a hot, lengthy and back-breaking job, and the whole business of laundering demanded great reserves of strength and energy.

Added to this was the consideration that clothes had to last. They were complicated to make and the expense of providing them had to be justified by years of use. The Victorians loved to keep up appearances, but they could not tolerate waste. There might even be a certain perverse pride in this enforced economy: 'Other women, if they liked, might have their best thread-lace in every wash, but when Mrs Glegg died, it would be found that she had better lace laid by in the right hand drawer of her wardrobe, in the Spotted Chamber, than ever Mrs Wooll of St Ogg's had bought in her life, although Mrs Wooll wore her lace before it was paid for.'[2] Not surprisingly, then, clothes care developed into a fine art, and hints were lovingly handed on from housewife to housewife.

The middle-class housewife of the late nineteenth century was in a difficult position. Her formal education had almost certainly placed more emphasis on accomplishments than on domestic economy, and if she had been sent away to school she had not even assisted her mother at home. Upon getting married, she was suddenly expected not only to supervise the running of her home, but to participate in it to an extent that her mother had never had to. Such servants as she might be able to find would be conscious of their own scarcity value, and almost certainly temperamental and hard to please. No wonder she felt bewildered. Her plight was acknowledged in many of the magazines of the period: 'The first year of married life, which, surely, should be a happy, contented one, is far too often marred by "those dreadful servants". Angelina does not know how to manage them, and meets Edwin day after day with red eyes. Edwin says soothingly, "Never mind, my darling", kisses her, fondly listening for three hundred consecutive times, perhaps, with the most perfect good-humour and sympathy to her complaints. But, breakers ahead! at the three hundred and first time, Edwin, to Angelina's unmitigated astonishment and indignation, loses a little of his evenness of temper when listening to the usual heartrending recital of his wife's woes, and actually frowns. . . . Angelina has discovered that her husband can be very ill-tempered when he likes, and Edwin's visions of happiness get dimmed, and all because his wife's education was "all drawing room and no kitchen".'[3] Happily, however, the magazines did not merely lament such a situation, but set about to rectify it.

Women's magazines had first been published as early as the seventeenth century, but initially, owing to the expense of production and the small reading public, they had catered only for a tiny handful of leisured middle- and upper-class women, and consisted chiefly of fashion news and romantic fiction. During the middle of the nineteenth century they became rather more practical, featuring cookery recipes and needlework patterns, the prime example being the outstandingly successful *The English-woman's Domestic Magazine,* launched in 1852 by Mrs Beeton's husband, and reflecting her preoccupation with household management. In the last quarter of the century, such magazines proliferated at a tremendous rate, and their circulation increased likewise. Widespread literacy was one of the most obvious causes, while better communications ensured wider distribution, and cheaper paper and improved printing techniques lowered the cost and made such luxuries available far lower down the social scale. Thus *Home Notes* (1894) and *Home Chat* (1895) were brought out with a specifically lower-middle-class readership in mind.[4]

Here then was the answer to the bewildered housewife's prayer. The magazine took on the role of the experienced friend and mentor. In its pages the details of household management were clearly set out, whole series of articles being devoted to laundry work or baby care, and the ignorant housewife could even write in to the Exchange columns with a specific enquiry, confident that she would get her answer in the next issue. Nor need she even feel embarrassed at revealing her ignorance, for the columns were run on a strictly anonymous basis, all contributors adopting an appropriate pseudonym, such as 'Newly Married' or 'Humble Bee'.

In one respect at least the Victorian housewife scored over her modern counterpart. She knew exactly what her clothes were made of, and could adjust her cleaning methods accordingly. Nowadays, with the bewildering proliferation of man-made fibres, few of them identifiable by the naked eye, it is difficult to imagine a time when all fabrics were necessarily wool, linen, cotton or silk, or a mixture of these. But it certainly simplified the process of cleaning. Furthermore, all Victorian girls of whatever social status were taught needlework from a very early age, as innumerable samplers testify, and this gave them a sound understanding of, and a sensitive feeling for, textiles of any kind. Thus the Victorian woman's attitude to clothes care was intelligent and informed.

The lengths to which our great-grandmothers went to preserve their clothes seems nothing short of incredible to our labour-saving times. Dresses were carefully unpicked before washing, and sewn up again afterwards; while drying, lace was held in position by hundreds of pins, because ironing would have flattened it and thus spoiled its appearance; the housewife even made her own soap and blacking, and everybody learned how to clean silk dresses that could not be washed. By the end of the century, however, there are signs that this state of things is on the wane. The magazines contain increasing numbers of advertisements for patent bleaches, soaps and shoe-polishes, and by the First World War the simplification of costume and the advent of ready-to-wear clothing had sown the seeds of today's 'throw-away' attitude to clothes.

In this book we aim to describe the sort of clothing which our great-grandmothers had to clean, and to give details of the methods they used. To this end, we have taken a typical basic wardrobe and allotted a separate chapter to each type of garment, first describing the nature of the garment and giving a brief summary of the changing styles during the Victorian period, and then going on to recount the most popular recipes and techniques for cleaning and day-to-day maintenance. A separate chapter on storage explains how clothes were preserved and cared for when not in use.

All the recipes mentioned in *Crinolines and Crimping Irons* were intended for use on 'natural' fabrics – silk, cotton, linen or wool – and materials. None of them were intended for use on modern synthetic fabrics. In addition, old, historic fabrics deteriorate over the years, and old stains undergo chemical changes. We must therefore advise extreme caution before using one of these recipes today for either a fresh stain on a modern material or an old stain on an old material. We have discussed this problem more fully in Appendix 1.

Notes and References

1   *Cassell's Family Magazine*, 1876.

2   George Eliot, *The Mill on the Floss*, 1860.

3   *Sylvia's Home Journal*, 1878.

4   For a full treatment of this subject, see Cynthia White, *Women's Magazines, 1693-1968*, 1970.

I

Dresses

1 The Changing Styles

The reign of Queen Victoria spanned sixty-four years, from 1837 to 1901. During this time women's fashions passed through many variations. Skirts expanded and deflated, waistlines rose and fell with the decades, but some features remained constant throughout the period. Skirts, for example, never rose much above the ankle, and although evening dress was often quite revealing, during the daytime sleeves were always long and necklines comparatively high.

Materials, too, remained fairly constant, for artificial fibres were as yet unknown, and all garments were made of silk, wool, cotton, linen, or a mixture of these. In general, silk was worn for formal occasions, linen and cotton for informal summer wear and wool for winter. Changes in style found more obvious expression in the shape of the dress, the patterns and colours of the fabrics and the type of trimmings. It is also true to say that all garments in the first half of the Victorian period were completely hand-sewn. The sewing machine appeared in 1846, but it was not until the mid 'sixties that clothing was generally machine made, and even after this time some dresses were wholly or partly hand-sewn.

1837-40

At the time of Queen Victoria's accession to the throne, fashion favoured a soft and pretty look, with full, floor-length skirts and a bodice shaped to the figure. Necklines were usually V-shaped or comparatively low, and often trimmed with a collar of white lace or muslin. This was either detachable, or part of the chemisette, a kind of sleeveless bodice, usually muslin, worn underneath the dress. Sleeves were long, and often gathered on the upper arm and wrist, with a slight fullness at the elbow, this being the last vestige of the 'gigot' or 'leg of mutton' sleeves of the early 1830s. Bodices fastened at the back with hooks and eyes, or eyelet holes, and were usually lined with plain cotton or linen. To achieve the fashionable small waist, a boned corset was worn, and the dress bodice was shaped to this by means of a centre front seam, and two darts under the bust. In many cases these darts and seams were also boned, the bones being inserted into the lining.

The skirt was made from several widths of material, pleated to the bodice at the front and sides, and gathered, to give extra fullness, at the back. Since most skirts were lined with a fairly stout material, such as glazed cotton, and worn over several petticoats, the effect was a dome-like silhouette, with the extra fullness at the back supported on a small bustle in the form of down-filled pads or layers of starched cotton, tied with a tape round the waist. In many cases the dress was topped with a little cape called a pelerine, made either of white muslin or in the same material as the dress. This garment gave extra width across the shoulders and provided a contrast to the tiny waist.

The softness of the line was reflected in the fabrics. Cotton and muslin were very popular, but perhaps the most characteristic material of the late 'thirties was 'challis'. This had a silk warp and a wool weft, so combining both lightness and softness. These fabrics were usually printed with flowers, twigs or abstract patterns on a white or cream background, and tiny stippled dots were used to give hazy patches of colour.

For evening wear, however, silk was the usual fabric. The late 'thirties and early 'forties saw an attempt to revive styles from earlier centuries. Pointed waists 'in the antique style' were all the rage, and heavily brocaded silks, usually with coloured flowers on a cream background, were inspired by eighteenth-century fabrics. In some cases original eighteenth-century gowns were rescued from wardrobes and attics and adapted to suit current styles. They followed the same lines as day dresses, but with tight-fitting, pointed bodices, short sleeves, and a very low décolletage, trimmed with a deep lace collar or 'bertha'.

1840-50

The 1840s saw a revival of Gothic forms, as expressed in the pinnacles and slender pointed arches of Victorian Gothic buildings, and women's fashions reflected this style. Waists became longer and narrower. The dress bodice was brought down to a sharp point at the front, so that the upper half of the body formed a narrow inverted triangle. This line was usually emphasized by flat pleats, set in converging lines down the bodice front. A softer version of this style appeared after 1843, consisting of a loose panel of material pleated to the shoulders and gathered at the centre front waist, so forming a shape like a half-open fan.

The total silhouette was also an elongated triangle. The head was small and neat, the face framed by a close-fitting bonnet; the shoulders drooped, the arms were virtually pinned to the side of the body by low-set sleeves, which were usually long and tight; and from the low waistline the skirt spread out to form the base of the triangle. Skirts had now grown much fuller, requiring far more fabric, so that we are told, in 1842, that Lady Aylesbury 'wears forty-eight yards of material in each of her gowns,'[1] and some skirts reached four to five yards round the hem. In order to achieve this, while avoiding bulky gathers at the waist, the material was now gauged rather than pleated, that is, the dress and its lining were folded into tight organ pleats, and sewn to the bodice at each alternate fold. 'By this means that excessive fullness which would be otherwise disposed of in gathers or pleats is formed exactly to the shape.'[2] To fill out this wider skirt, linen or cotton petticoats were worn, many of them stiffened with cording, and additional support was supplied by a horsehair petticoat or 'crinoline'.

Fabrics were usually plain, for both day and evening wear, the favourite being the 'changeable' or shot silks in subtle shades of green, mauve or brown. Soft woollen fabrics, such as cashmere and merino, were also used for day dresses, and were often printed with small floral patterns or stripes. Other popular designs were copied from contemporary shawls, for this was a period when the fringed silk and wool shawls of Norwich and Paisley, themselves copies of imported Indian designs, were almost universally worn. Enveloping the upper half of the body, and disguising the shoulder line, these shawls also helped to produce the triangular silhouette which was the chief feature of mid-Victorian women's dress.

The overall effect was neat and subdued, the general outline uncluttered by trimmings or ornament. In day dresses, velvet ribbons, pleats, or ruched bands of material traced a V-shape on the bodice, and this was sometimes mirrored by diverging lines of trimming on the skirt. The wrists and neck were finished with neat white undersleeves and collar, usually part of the chemisette, but sometimes separate: 'For morning wear collarettes of English embroidery, composed of cambric, are most in vogue, beautifully worked with the needle.'[3] Otherwise, the chief concessions to ornament were lines of piping at the seams. These could be single or double, and were usually in the same material as the dress, or in similar colours, but they were functional as well as decorative, stiffening the seams and giving greater definition to the different parts of the dress. After 1843, flounces began to appear on evening dresses, and, by the end of the decade, on day dresses too, heralding a major style of the 1850s. In general, however, the dresses of the 1840s were plain and sober.

1850-56

In the 1850s, styles became softer and more decorative. The shape was still triangular, but with the emphasis on the horizontal rather than the vertical lines. As early as 1846, the separate bodice and skirt had made its first appearance, and by 1851 this style had largely superseded the all-in-one dress. The most usual form was the jacket bodice, fastening down the front, often with decorative buttons of pearl or gilt. The neckline was still high, or with a V-neck filled by a chemisette, but the material now extended over the hips in the form of basques, thus blurring the line of the waist. The

long front bones of the 1840s bodice disappeared and were replaced, if at all, by two pairs of shorter bones, thus raising the waist
and placing much less restriction on the wearer. This style became
typical of the 'fifties and, even where the back-fastening bodice was
retained, it often adopted the basques of the jacket bodice.

Sleeves followed the same pattern, the narrow sleeve of the
'forties giving way to fuller, looser styles. The most usual form was
called the 'pagoda' sleeve and this retained the narrow upper arm,
but spread to a very wide opening, and by 1857 the sleeve was in
fact a square of material, pleated to the armhole, and allowed to
hang open. An alternative form, the 'bishop' sleeve, appeared in
the mid 'fifties. This was made from two sections of material,
pleated or gathered to the armhole, from which the material spread
out, but was caught in again, and pleated or gathered at the wrist.

This pattern of expansion was most obvious in the skirt, however. A separate skirt was worn with the jacket bodice, and the
material pleated, or gathered, if the fabric was light, on to a
separate waistband. This skirt grew steadily wider throughout the
1850s. It still retained the stiffened lining, but, in addition, more
and more petticoats were used to fill it out. As many as six or seven
were worn at one time, including corded cotton and horsehair, and
the heat and weight of such a burden can hardly be imagined
today.

Even the design and fabric of the skirt were used to give an
impression of greater width. We have seen that flounces were introduced in the late 'forties, but they really came into their own in the
1850s, so that by 1853, 'Flounces are very generally worn; on all
thin materials they are indispensable.'[4] For while the basic skirt was
held out as far as possible by the numerous petticoats, the successive
layers of gathered flounces set onto it increased the circumference
still further. Where jacket bodices were worn, the basques formed
yet another flounce over the hips. In many cases, these skirt
flounces were woven, printed, or embroidered 'à disposition', that
is horizontally, so that the bands of pattern lay across the width of
the skirt, and gave still greater emphasis to the horizontal line.

The higher waist, full sleeves and flounced skirt produced a silhouette in which curves and angles were blurred and softened, and
trimmings were used to increase this effect. Fringing appeared on
silk and woollen dresses, tracing a wide V-shape on the front of the
bodice, and edging the sleeves. Flounces were used for sleeves as

well as skirts, and skirt flounces were often pinked and scalloped at the edges. Collars and undersleeves were still worn, the latter expanding with the sleeve of the dress, and adding yet another flounce in the form of a frill at the wrist.

Fabrics, too, were brighter in colour, and velvet-figured silk was a new and richer fabric. For day wear a favourite material was white checked muslin, printed with flowers or 'Paisley' cone patterns in one, or occasionally two colours, such as pink and mauve. Silks, too, were figured with checks and flowers, and printed patterns were softened by using different shades of the same colour, so that forms blended into one another. Another means of softening patterns was by printing only the warp threads of a fabric before weaving, and leaving the weft threads plain, so that the areas of colour were broken and lightened. Warp-printed flowers were popular for skirt flounces in the early years of the decade, and helped to increase the general effect of blurred pattern and silhouette.

Evening dresses retained their low curving necklines, draped with lace, but many bodices were now pointed at both front and back. As bodices and skirts were usually separate, many thrifty women had their skirts made with two bodices, one for day and one for evening wear.

1856-70

Throughout the early 'fifties, skirts grew wider, and the layers of petticoats increased until they reached a point where the very weight of the petticoats, one on top of the other, prevented them from filling out the skirt any further. Then it seemed that fashions must change, and in 1856 the solution appeared. The hooped petticoat, not seen since the eighteenth century, was rediscovered.

This hooped petticoat, or 'cage', consisted of a linen or cotton petticoat into which circles of whalebone were inserted. These were soon replaced, however, by steel, and then watchspring, which was more flexible. The advantage of the cage was that it could support even the widest skirt, thus doing away with the need for layers of heavy petticoats. Not surprisingly, it soon caught on and adopted the name 'crinoline' from the horsehair petticoat which it superseded.

Fashion. of the late 'fifties and early 'sixties were greatly influenced by this in a few important ways. Skirts of five or six yards round the hem could be distended to their full circumference when supported on this structure, and the female silhouette was transformed into a wide-based pyramid. Admittedly, the majority of women, judging by contemporary photographs, kept their skirts to a reasonable size, but the wits and cartoonists of the day found sufficient examples to inspire numerous jokes and lampoons on the excesses of the crinoline. We read humorous accounts of ladies falling off bridges and parachuting to safety by means of their full skirts, or being kept afloat in water, the crinoline acting as a lifebuoy. It was said to be impossible to pass through a doorway, or even down a staircase, at the same time as a crinolined lady, and gentlemen were advised to shin up lamposts if they wished to reach out over their lady's skirt and take her by the hand. Even the wearers had to admit that there were disadvantages: 'To walk with so immense a paraphernalia around one was not very easy; and the slender bust, placed in the centre of this volume of material, appeared to be detached from the rest of the body altogether. To be able to sit so as not to cause the rebellious springs to fly open, required a miracle of precision. To get into a carriage without rumpling the delicate fabrics – for evening toilettes were made of tulle and lace – required a great deal of time, much quietness on the part of the horses and patience on the part of the fathers and husbands, whose complaisance was put to an enormous test, compelled as they were to remain motionless in the midst of these "images fragiles".'[5]

The crinoline was not only impractical, but in some cases positively dangerous, for it was extremely difficult to control a large and buoyant crinoline skirt, and there are many reports of them being set alight by the open fires of the day, and, without the layers of petticoats to protect them, many ladies were badly burned.

There were some advantages to the fashion, however. Aunt Etty in Gwen Raverat's *Period Piece* was much in favour of the crinoline. ' "Oh it was delightful!" she said. "I've never been so comfortable since they went out. It kept your petticoats away from your legs and made walking so light and easy".' It eased the waistline, too, for the huge skirt made any waist look small by comparison. Thus, corsets were loosened and shortened, and tight, pointed bodices were discarded in favour of short bodices, with a horizontal waistline just above the natural level.

The crinoline also affected the construction of the skirt, and, within a few years, gores[6] were introduced, thus allowing the skirt to follow the pyramidal shape of the crinoline. Flounces were discarded, since it was no longer necessary to resort to optical illusion to increase the width of the skirt. A single flounce at the hem was all that was needed to give a flowing line. Otherwise, skirts were generally plain.

The crinoline continued to dominate fashion until the mid 'sixties, but during the early years of the decade it had already begun to change its form, flattening at the front to leave the fullness concentrated at the back. At this time the dress usually consisted of a short, front-fastening bodice with a round neck, bishop sleeves and, in many cases, long basques at the back. The skirt was gored at front and sides, and pleated or gathered at the back, the extra fullness extending into a slight train. Woollen braid was added to the hem, to protect it from dirt and wear. Silk was the most usual fabric for these dresses; plain, corded or watered for daytime, and light silks and silk muslins for evening.

At the same time, the 'sixties saw a growing interest in outdoor pursuits such as walking and croquet. Naturally, silk dresses with trains were impractical for such pastimes, and a range of informal wear was introduced to the fashion scene. Matching skirts and jackets, or capes, in wool or linen, were worn over white chemisettes and finished with a deep pointed Swiss belt, so providing the beginnings of the tailored suit. Special walking skirts were also designed; these could be hitched up, by means of cords, lifting the hem clear of the mud. These leisure clothes were usually made in the stouter wools, linens and cottons, and were often very brightly coloured, black, white and scarlet being a favourite combination.

In fact, fabrics in general were more brightly coloured in the 1860s, for the new aniline dyes were beginning to replace the traditional vegetable dyes, and silk dresses appeared in such startling shades as magenta and solferino. Trimmings added to the effect. Linear patterns of black braid appeared on summer dresses of white linen or cotton piqué. Black lace, often machine-made, was much used on pale evening dresses, and sometimes on day wear, and the reverse combination of white lace on dark materials was also popular. Whatever their colour, formal dresses were never complete without full white undersleeves and, in many cases, white linen collars and white muslin cravats.

By 1865 the skirt was almost completely flat at the front, and the aim was to give a smooth line over the hips. This produced the Princess style, by which the dress was cut without a waist seam. In 1867 the following instructions were given for converting a formal Princess dress into a walking dress: 'Out of doors the long dress can be converted into a short dress by pulling the fullness of the skirt to the back and pinning the side breadths together behind; the rest of the fullness is pulled through the loop thus made.'[7] The effect was to produce a bustle-like mound of fabric at the back, and this was the pattern which the crinoline was destined to follow.

One development of the hitched-up walking skirt was a form of double skirt which appeared in both formal and evening dresses in the late 'sixties. The overskirt, which was shorter than the foundation skirt, was usually attached to a separate waistband, and was often looped up at the sides to form an apron shape in front and a large puff of material at the back. This was given further emphasis by a sash worn round the waist, whose large bow or tabs spread out over this puff. As the crinoline shrank to a half-crinoline or 'crinolette', supporting only the back of the skirt, tapes were sewn inside the overskirt, and these, when tied to the waist, pulled the material into a 'pannier puff'. To support this a bustle of hoops or horsehair was worn on top of the half-crinoline, and within a few years the crinoline had been discarded altogether, leaving only the bustle.

1870-80

This bustle of the early 1870s could be made from a variety of materials, including wire and horsehair flounces, but the general effect was always one of softly undulating curves. In many cases the back breadths of the skirt were cut longer than the rest, and much of the surplus material was pleated to the back side seams, then bunched together by tapes tied from these seams across the back of the skirt. Thus the front of the skirt was drawn more closely to the figure, while the material at the back puffed up from the waist and fell in a series of arcs and curves which finally subsided into a train. The overskirt was swathed across the front in the form of a decorative apron, and usually this, the underskirt, and all the other draperies were trimmed with layers of ruched and pleated flounces. 'What will characterise the present epoch in the history of Fashion is the amount of trimming with which we have found it possible to load every separate article.'[8] Machine lace and embroidery, and ready-made frills had already appeared in the late 1860s, but in the early 'seventies they really came into their own, and necklines, bodice fronts and sleeves were lavishly trimmed with lace, velvet ribbon and fringing. Colours were soft and subtle, with a preference for pale shades such as grey and mauve, a darker shade of the predominant colour being used for the trimmings. Evening dresses in particular made great use of frills, flounces, ribbons, flowers and lace – 'It is impossible to put too many flounces, puffings and flowers on the tarlatan, gauze, grenadine or tulle skirts of ball dresses'[9] – and the overall effect was of a frothy cloud of fabric.

After 1873, tapes were attached to the side seams of the skirt in order to draw the fullness to the back, and consequently the dress began to fit still more closely to the front of the body. The bodice had already begun to lengthen during the first few years of the decade, and by 1873 it came right down over the hips and was christened the 'cuirasse' bodice, because it fitted so closely to the figure. The emphasis was now on the vertical line, and sleeves too became long and narrow, and were often made in a different material or colour from the bodice, which thus appeared even narrower. With this new vertical emphasis, the bustle began to diminish and the fullness at the back of the skirt was redistributed in the form of a long train.

By the mid 'seventies the fashionable dress had become sheath-like, producing a style that was one of the most restricting in the history of women's fashions. The bodice was usually high-necked, or if V-necked was filled by a chemisette or a section of dress material with a high collar. The bodice fitted the figure like a glove, extending right down over the hips and necessitating a corset longer and tighter than that of any previous fashion. Even the sleeves were tight, and restricted the movement of the arms. Beneath the bodice the separate skirt was gored at the front and sides to fit snugly over the hips, and as all the fullness was tied to the back, the material clung to the legs, so that the wearer was virtually hobbled. As one writer complained, 'our skirts are now so tight that our sitting and walking are seriously inconvenienced.'[10] The back widths of the skirt were formed into a deep box pleat, held together by the tapes inside, and dragged behind as a long and heavy 'fishtail' train, which was supported on a demi-petticoat of stiffened muslin. Many trains were detachable, fastening on to the body of the skirt with metal hooks, and were partly protected from dirt and wear by a pleated frill of muslin, known as a balayeuse, attached to the inside of the hem. They were, nevertheless, extremely inconvenient, for while walking 'They must be held up with one hand, or they may be thrown à l'Amazone over one arm.'[11] And when sitting, 'care must be exercised not to sit upon the back breadths; the train must be brought to the left before sitting down.'[12] Considering that the most popular colour for these trained dresses of 1876 was cream, it was altogether a thoroughly uncomfortable and impractical style.

The new fashion demanded clinging fabrics that fitted closely to the figure, so woollens came into favour, although satins, silk and cottons were also used for day wear, and satins, velvets, muslins and brocades for evening. Cheaper versions of these fabrics also appeared, in the form of velveteen and sateen. In many cases the vertical silhouette was emphasized by the use of two different materials, or two different colours, a darker shade being used for the centre back and front panels of the bodice. Poplin and velvet were frequently mixed, and wool was combined with silk, even for evening dresses.

To add further complications trimmings and draperies were more lavish than ever, and in 1876 we are told: 'It is now quite impossible to describe dresses with exactitude; the skirts are draped so mysteriously, the arrangement of trimmings is usually one-sided and the fastenings are so curiously contrived that after studying any particular toilette for even quarter of an hour the task of writing down how it is all made remains hopeless.'[13] The material of the skirt was arranged in narrow, closely pleated flounces, draped folds, and lines of puffing, while bodices and skirts were trimmed with velvet, silk ribbons, bows, ruching, fringing, feathers, lace and embroidery. Seventy to eighty yards of trimming might be employed on a skirt alone, and evening wear added tinsel, sequins and beads to this complex array, so that 'A modern ballroom looks like an assemblage of stage queens covered with paste and spangles.'[14]

1880-90

Between 1875 and 1879 the drapery on the front of the skirt was again arranged in the form of an apron, and the emphasis was once more returning to width across the hips. After 1878, short trainless walking dresses appeared, and by 1880 the train was almost completely banished for daytime. Without the weight of the train pulling it back, the skirt now fell in a straight vertical tube. This was often trimmed with horizontal bands of pleating and ruching, and with draped panniers over the hips. This emphasis on the hips soon led, as it had done in the early 'seventies, to fullness at the back, so that the early 'eighties saw the return of the bustle. This reached its maximum size in the middle of the decade, and did not disappear completely until 1889. It was different from the bustle of the 'seventies, however, in that it was narrower, and took a central position, rather than spreading round the hips. It was also more angular, jutting out from the body like a shelf, and, since the skirts of the 'eighties were shorter and lacked the train of the seventies, the skirt fell sharply from the angle of the bustle and hung in an unhindered vertical line. The bustle consisted usually of a pad or cushion, often sewn into the back of the skirt, below which hung rows of semi-circular steel bands. In many cases these were inserted into the skirt itself, lying flat when the dress was in storage, and pulled into shape by means of tapes when the dress was worn.

The bodice remained tight-fitting for the rest of the 'eighties, and was made of numerous shaped sections, each boned at the seams. In the middle years it was long and pointed at both front and back. A stand-up collar was added, and by 1885 this had become the high 'officer' collar. Long, tight sleeves completed this rigid vertical silhouette.

During this period of the bustle, the complexity of the skirt increased, until it consisted of little more than a foundation skirt smothered in applied draperies and trimmings. In the early 'eighties, these consisted chiefly of pleated flounces and bands of puffing, but by the middle of the decade many skirts fell in vertical pleats, with draperies swathed across them to give the impression of an overskirt or apron. By the end of the 'eighties, however, there was a fashion for asymmetrical draperies – 'Skirts now never have two sides alike'[15] – and it was quite possible to find a skirt composed of seven or eight sections, each of which was of a different shape and construction from the rest.

The harsher angles and more sculptural draperies of this decade were made possible by the use of heavier fabrics, such as thick woollens, serge, brocaded silks and satins, velvet and plush, and stronger colours and colour contrasts, such as dark brown and blue, and dark reds and purples, gave greater definition to the shape.

The 1880s was a period of economic depression, and this is reflected in the greater use of inferior fabrics. In fact, the elaborate construction of the skirts may well have been intended to proclaim a financial status which is belied by the quality of the materials and the workmanship. Whatever the reason, velveteen and sateen were favourite materials for day dresses.

Evening dresses retained the draperies of day dresses until 1887, when a new style appeared in which skirts were vertically pleated, and the décolletage supported only by shoulder straps. They were still trained, however, and extremely elaborate. Figured silks and brocades, velvet and plush were often mixed together, displaying such alarming colour combinations as pink and red, pink and yellow, or scarlet and green. As for the trimmings, these included lace, chenille fringe, pearls, sequins, bows, frills, feathers, and even whole stuffed birds, while real or imitation insects and animals were a characteristic feature of the decade. A ball dress of 1886 is described thus: 'The skirt of white tulle with pointed tulle tunic having a design of briar roses in satin. In the corner the outline of a bird's nest with pearl eggs and butterflies. Low satin bodice with tulle bertha ornamented with a spray of wild roses.'[16]

Perhaps in reaction to these elaborate confections, the 'eighties also saw a trend towards simplicity in the form of the tailor-made suit. Tailor-made jackets and matching skirts, in heavy cloth and tweeds, were fashionable in the early 'eighties for the country and for travelling, but by 1889 versions in smoother fabrics were worn as fashionable day dress. Their jackets were cut like the dress bodice, but with collars and revers, and were worn over a blouse or waistcoat. Their influence was felt even in dresses, many of which were given revers and false fronts, or 'plastrons', in imitation of the tailor-made, and by 1886, 'All elaborate frillings and puffings are fast disappearing in favour of straight falling lines.'[17]

1890-1901

In 1889 the bustle disappeared, and with it the complex draperies of the skirt. The skirt of the 1890s fitted closely over the hips, shaped by gores and darts, and fell in straight folds, the fullness still at the centre back, but now without any substructure or support. In this decade it was the bodice which was the centre of attention. Usually fastening at the front, and displaying a high, stiff collar, the bodice was still heavily boned. During the first two or three years, the vertical emphasis was retained in a low waistline, long narrow revers or V-shaped trimming on the front, and a kick-up at the head of the sleeves. After 1893, however, the emphasis became more horizontal. Waists narrowed; skirts widened at the hem, reaching a width of five and a half yards; and sleeves swelled at the upper arm until, by 1896, they had developed into the huge gigot sleeves which were one of the characteristic features of this decade. Everything was calculated to increase the width of the shoulder line, so emphasizing the tiny waist. Revers broadened, and square, V-shaped, or round yokes were traced with frills or bands of trimming.

Evening dresses followed the same pattern. The sleeves were shorter, ending on or above the elbow, but they grew, just like those of the day dresses, and still greater width was given by epaulettes or a bertha of lace across the neckline.

The 1890s were also notable for the further development of the tailor-made. In previous decades this had consisted of a dress and jacket, or a bodice and skirt and waistcoat, but it was in the 'nineties that the form of blouse, skirt and jacket was first adopted, and the separate blouse and skirt accepted as fashionable wear for every day. In achieving this status, however, the blouse had lost something of its informality. 'Blouses have grown so much in popular favour during the last few years that from négligée garments of the loosest, baggiest and most unpretentious description they have developed into the favourite bodices of the age, . . . so much caught down and pleated and pressed into shape upon a close fitting lining that their leading characteristics have almost disappeared.'[18]

The most popular materials of the first half of the 'nineties were tweeds, corduroys and heavy cloths for tailor-mades, which were

Day and evening dresses, 1846. Daytime gowns and bonnets are neat and demure, ounces are reserved for the evening. Note the elaborate morning and evening caps at the p. (*The World of Fashion*)

2 Men's day dress, 1851. Dark frock coats compliment light trousers and starched whit
collars. (*Gentleman's Magazine*)

decorated with braiding and velvet appliqué. For more formal wear, heavily brocaded silks and satins were preferred, and lace was used for sleeve flounces and berthas. Colours were bright, and strong contrasts, such as black and white, and yellow and red, were much in favour.

After 1897, however, styles changed, preparing the way for the fashions of the early 1900s. Skirts lengthened so that they had to be held up while walking, and trains were revived for carriage dress. Skirts fitted more closely over the hips, and the introduction of secondary gores and insertions at the hem, supported by a flounced silk foundation skirt, produced a flowing, bell-shaped line. Sleeves finally deflated, leaving just a puff at the shoulder, and the silhouette was now one of gently flowing curves.

The change of mood was reflected in the choice of fabrics. 'All clinging materials will be used and even cloth will be of a soft texture.'[19] Soft wools, such as cashmere and mohair, were used for tailor-mades; clinging *crêpe de Chine* or wool muslin for day; and for evening dresses, 'Everything is veiled or trimmed with chiffon, jewelled net, the flimsiest of gauzes.'[20] The evening dresses were shaped and moulded to the figure by rows of pin tucks, and trimmed with lace and chiffon frills. The fabrics themselves, in cream or pastel shades, were embroidered or printed with meandering floral patterns, and warp-printing was revived again to blur and soften printed silks.

The last years of Victoria's reign, like the first, saw the modulation of a strident and exaggerated style into one that was soft and feminine. Thus, when Queen Victoria died in 1901, the styles of the Edwardian era were already prepared.

2 Care and Cleaning

The Victorian woman was faced with a difficult task in keeping her dresses clean and fresh. In the first place, very few of them were made of washable fabrics, and commercial dry-cleaners were unknown except for specialized items such as fur or lace. She was therefore dependent on her own resources. To make it worse, the fashions throughout the period were such as to encourage dirt –

skirts were floor-length and frequently trained, so that dirt accumulated in the hems – and the atmosphere, at least in urban areas, suffered from a degree of industrial pollution infinitely beyond today's level. Thus a report of 1850 describes how 'soon after daybreak, the great factory shafts beside the river begin to discharge immense volumes of smoke; their clouds soon become confluent; the sky is overcast with a dingy veil; the house-chimneys presently add their contributions; and by ten o'clock, as one approaches London from any hill in the suburbs, one may observe the total result of this gigantic nuisance hanging over the City like a pall.'[21] Nothing could be more misguided, however, than to suppose that the Victorian housewife had a low standard of cleanliness in her clothes; on the contrary, she was scrupulous to a degree bordering on fanaticism. We who throw our clothes into a washing machine or hand them over to a cleaner can hardly imagine the thoroughness with which our great-grandmothers examined every stain, every mark, before diagnosing the problem and applying a suitable remedy. If their zeal seems excessive, we must remind ourselves that their clothes had to last for a long time. Today's casual attitude to clothes would have astounded and shocked them.

Victorian dresses suffered remarkably little, in fact, from body dirt. This was chiefly because of the huge quantities of underwear worn. A dress worn over a chemise, a camisole and several petticoats, was effectively protected from contact with the body. Vulnerable points such as neck and wrists were safeguarded by detachable collars, cuffs and undersleeves which were removed for frequent washing. In addition to this, dress preservers made of rubber or chamois leather were in use from the beginning of the 1840s. A young girl enquiring about the perspiration problem in the 1850s was no doubt crushed on being told: 'My love, the perfect lady does *not* perspire,'[22] but the next generation, who placed more faith in scientific preparations than in gentility, had their own deodorants. Thus *Health, Beauty & The Toilet,* published in 1886 by 'A Lady Doctor', recommends a solution of chloride of lime and carbonate of soda, or a mixture of powdered salicylic acid, talc and starch.

If the Victorian dress was preserved from body dirt, it was nevertheless subjected to external soiling. Here again the careful housewife preferred preventive measures where possible. A magazine of 1883 listed a few of the ways in which clothes could be preserved:

'In sitting down, the best position is naturally taken to save flounces, frills, and sashes from creasing, and iron and cane open-work seats must be carefully eschewed, if the dress be of velvet, velveteen, or silk. The back of the chair, if of wood and varnished, must be remembered, as all materials grow shiny by rubbing on a hard substance. A white-washed or coloured wall will sometimes work great havoc with a dress; a danger which should be remembered at church, and in all kitchens and passages. . . . As a matter of economy, the dress should always be changed in the evening, and the walking dress brushed and laid by. . . . Handles of doors, arms of chairs, and ornaments of all kinds that stick out, must be remembered, and nails in the floors and stairs are inimical to tidy dresses. Never do anything in a violent hurry, nor with a sudden and jerky movement – you will not only look ungraceful, but you will tear some part of your apparel for certain.' [23]

Clearly then the Victorian woman was constantly aware of her clothes and the dangers that they were facing, and took every possible precaution to safeguard them. When, despite all her care, they needed cleaning, she might be able to wash them. The cotton and linen dresses that were in favour for daytime wear on and off throughout the period would not shrink or lose their texture if immersed in water, but washing was nevertheless a complicated procedure. Unlike silk and wool, linen and cotton are not naturally receptive to dyes, and during the nineteenth century colour fixing in these fabrics was unreliable. In washing a dress, therefore, you risked losing the dye along with the dirt. The magazines are full of hints for preventing this. Coloured muslin dresses could be treated with 'a little gall obtainable at the butcher's shop, and stirred into the wash-tub'.[24] This apparently helped to 'preserve treacherous, and brighten fast colours in all washable dresses.' A more dangerous measure required 'one pennyworth of sugar of lead . . . in a pail full of cold spring water. Put the dress into it, and let it remain there one hour. On taking it out, wash the dress as usual. I need scarcely remind "Emma W" that sugar of lead is a violent poison, and must be carefully used.' [25] Indeed we are reminded elsewhere that 'those using sugar of lead should be careful not to do so if they have any scratches, abrasions, or wounds about their hands.' [26] Another dangerous, but effective, substance was oil of vitriol, or sulphuric acid. Here the instructions for use are accompanied by

the caution that 'if washed at home, one of the ladies of the family
should go herself and put in the vitriol; as if trusted to the domestics
they may put in too much – in which case the dress will be destroyed by dropping all to pieces. It is well to have neither vitriol,
soda, nor pearl-ash kept in the kitchen. When necessary to use any
of these articles, let one of the ladies add them herself, as they are
all injurious if employed injudiciously, or in too large a quantity.'[27]

Different colours evidently required different fixatives: 'For buff
and cream-coloured alpaca or cashmere, mix in the wash and rinse
two-pennyworth of friar's balsam for one skirt. For black materials,
for one dress, two-pennyworth of ammonia in the wash and rinse.
For violet, ammonia or a small quantity of soda in the rinsing
water. There are some violets and mauves that fade in soda. For
green, vinegar in the rinse, in the proportion of two table-spoonfuls
of vinegar to a quart of rinse. For blue, to one dress, a good handful of common salt in the rinse. For brown and grey, ox-gall. For
white, blue the water with laundry blue.'[28] And elsewhere we are
told that 'when black or navy blue linens are washed, soap should
not be used. Take instead two potatoes grated into tepid soft water
(after having them washed and peeled), into which a teaspoonful
of ammonia has been put. Wash the linen with this, and rinse them
in cold blue water. They will need no starch, and should be dried
and ironed on the wrong side. An infusion of hay will keep the
natural colour in buff linens, and an infusion of bran will do the
same for brown linens and prints.'[29] Black pepper was recommended as a fixative for black calico or cambric, and to wash print
dresses: 'take three large handfuls of fresh green ivy leaves (well
washed), one quart of bran, and a quarter of a pound of common
yellow soap; boil all together till the soap is quite dissolved, strain,
and leave till cold; then add the liquid to as small a quantity of
water as possible for washing the dress. After being once washed
thus the colour is fixed.'[30] Even then your troubles might not be
over, for 'some colours, (pinks and light greens particularly,)
though they may stand perfectly well in washing, will change as
soon as a warm iron is applied to them; the pink turning purplish,
and the green bluish.'[31] Evidently there was no remedy for this,
and ladies were advised to obtain and test a sample of any fabric
before they bought it.

If the fabric of the dress had any kind of stiffening in it, it was
likely that this would have disappeared in the wash. It therefore

had to be restored, for the styles in vogue throughout most of the period could not be achieved if made of too flimsy a material. Fine muslins, which required only a suspicion of stiffening, could be treated with isinglass, while 'coloured cotton dresses, the appearance of which is injured by the use of starch, can be stiffened by wringing out of sweet milk'.[32] A dark chintz or calico dress, being a less delicate affair, could be squeezed through 'a stiffening made of a piece of glue about the size of the palm of your hand, broken up and melted thoroughly by boiling it in a gallon of soft water, and then allowed to cool. . . . This process will be found superior to starching a dark cotton dress (particularly a mourning chintz,) as the starch is apt to give it a whitish mealy look.'[33]

If the dress was made of silk or velvet, or of some kinds of wool, it would not wash. Specific stains, such as grease, ink or rust, were identified and removed by the appropriate means, which are dealt with in Chapter 10. General soiling required different treatment.

The worst hazard a dress had to face was mud. Roads, particularly in country areas, were poor, and in towns the horse-drawn traffic, moving ceaselessly along often unpaved streets, did nothing to promote cleanliness. Taine, visiting England in the 1860s, speaks of the 'most execrable wallow of mud'[34] in the streets of London. Little children earned a precarious living by sweeping the streets in front of pedestrians, but the quantity of mud swept up by an average skirt every day must have been enormous, and its removal a major daily task. Black clothes could apparently be cleansed 'by rubbing the spots with a raw potato cut in half',[35] and French merino, which was a fine twilled wool sometimes mixed with silk, could be wiped with a weak solution of carbonate of soda. But the usual method was plain brushing, as Gwen Raverat remembers in her autobiography *Period Piece*: 'Round the bottom of these skirts I had, with my own hands, sewn two and a half yards of "brush braid", to collect the worst of the mud; for they inevitably swept the roads, however carefully I might hold them up behind. . . . Afterwards the crusted mud had to be brushed off, which might take an hour or more to do. There can be no more futile job, imposed by an idiotic convention, than that of perpetual skirt-brushing. This was the only work that ever made me wish that I had a maid. . . .'

If the dress was to be cleaned all over, there were various methods in use. One was to rub the fabric with a dry substance which would absorb any surface grease. Stale bread was recommended for this purpose, and if velvet was 'but very slightly soiled, brush it free of all dirt, and rub it gently with fine, dry bran, renewing the layer directly it looks soiled'.[36] Another method was to apply some kind of volatile liquid which would dissolve the dirt and evaporate very quickly – the same principle as dry-cleaning today. Velvet responded to benzine or turpentine 'rubbed on with a piece of clean flannel, taking care not to flatten the pile';[37] while for silk and wool either benzoin, an aromatic resin, or a mixture of 'one ounce of borax, one ounce of sal ammoniac, two ounces of ammonia dissolve[d] in six ounces of *hot* water'[38] were effective. The third method was to use a home-made product. A silk dress might be sponged over with 'a strong infusion of black tea'.[39] If its colour was light, thus rendering the tea treatment impossible, this improbable-sounding recipe could be 'used with impunity': 'Take 1 quart of lukewarm water, and mix it with 4 oz of soft soap, 4 oz of honey, and a good size wineglass of gin. The silk must be unpicked and laid in widths on a kitchen table; then take a common scrubbing brush (such as housemaids use), quite clean, dip it in the mixture and scrub the silk hard on both sides so as to saturate it. Rinse it in cold water twice until free from soap, hang it on a clothes horse to drain until half dry; then iron it. The silk when laid on the table must be kept quite smooth, so that every bit may come under the brush.'[40] Unpicking a dress completely before cleaning it seems to have been normal practice, though the complication of the styles must have made it a daunting task. Perhaps dresses were only subjected to this treatment when they were going to be restyled anyway. The use of gin as a cleaning agent, which seems alarmingly wasteful today, was in fact perfectly sensible: even in 1895, long after Gladstone's taxation of alcohol, Harrods were retailing gin at 1/6d a pint. Its effectiveness is attested by the fact that it recurs frequently as an ingredient of various cleaning fluids, and even simply mixed with egg-white to remove stains from silk. Other cleaning fluids included 'equal parts of alcohol and lukewarm water . . . cold coffee well strained, or water in which an old black kid glove has been boiled. This latter mixture is a glove put into a pint of water and boiled down to a half pint, or two gloves in a quart of water. Each and everyone of these fluids is excellent in effect. Sponge the goods on what will be the right side when made up, as some silks can be turned after being worn. Hang each piece on a line to drip; when nearly dry, but still quite damp, iron with a moderately warm iron on the wrong side, placing a piece of soft, black cambric or crinoline between the iron and the goods, and ironing each piece until it is perfectly dry. Then lay away the pieces without folding them. . . . The ironing must always be done on the wrong side and over a second fabric, which must be black if the material is dark coloured.'[41] Thus we see Mrs Gaskell's heroine Mary Barton, after the death of the impoverished Ben Davenport, 'busy planning how her old black gown (her best when her mother died) might be sponged, and turned, and lengthened into something like decent mourning for the widow.' Velvet, which obviously could not stand saturation by a cleaning fluid, 'may be cleaned by the aid of a bit of bacon rind and some crape; the former will take off all the dirt, and the latter is the best kind of brush.'[42]

Sometimes the colour or texture of a garment was impaired without its needing actual cleaning. For this eventuality too the Victorian housewife was prepared. Velvet could be freshened by the application with a stiff brush of 'a mixture composed of two tablespoonfuls of liquid ammonia and two of warm water. This must be well rubbed in, and will remove all stains and creases.'[43] Steaming, another method of restoring velvet, could be done by placing a wet cloth over a hot iron, 'but, aside from the fact that one may sit and do this, it is better to have the even cloud of steam from the top of a tea-kettle, or any other open vessel of water. There is less danger of marring the velvet by pressing the edges un-wittingly over the corners of the iron in such a way as to leave marks on the surface. It really takes two people "to make a good job of" restoring velvet in this home-made fashion. While one with both hands holds the material straight, and moves it slowly over the steaming surface, the other with a soft velvet brush should brush the pile in the right direction.'[44] Even the brushing had to be performed in a particular way: 'Take a hat-brush (not too soft, and having the bristles elastic, and returning at once to their original state after being pressed aside,) hold it firmly under the palm of the hand, in the direction of the arm, and with the bristles downward, and pressing them first gently into the substance of the velvet, then twist round the arm, hand, and brush all together, as on an axis, without moving them forward or backward. The foreign matters will thus be drawn up and flirted out of the flock without injury to the substance of the velvet, and the brush must be lifted up and placed in a similar manner over every part requiring to be brushed. By this means velvet will be improved instead of deteriorated, and will last for years.'[45] Plush, a similar fabric to velvet, very popular for dresses in the 'eighties and 'nineties, was evidently prone to fading, but 'after careful use an application of chloroform will bring out the colours as bright as ever'.[46] Faded cashmere was to be sponged with 'equal parts of alcohol and ammonia, diluted with a little warm water',[47] while black crape, lace or net could be 'dipped in water, coloured with the blue-bag, adding a lump of loaf sugar to stiffen, and pinned on to a newspaper on a bed'.[48]

Crape, the fabric which was extensively worn for mourning throughout the period, was a plain silk gauze, stiffened with shellac, and embossed by passing over a heated revolving copper cylinder engraved with a design. The process was a secret which Samuel Courtauld bought from the firm of Grout; it made his fortune at a time when the abolition of import duties on foreign silk was undermining the rest of the English silk industry. The rules of Victorian mourning etiquette ensured that a vast amount of crape was worn, but the fabric had one drawback: it soon lost its texture and went limp. Cecilia Ridley, writing in 1842, asks 'to have a good deal of black crape sent as it so soon gets shabby – perhaps thirteen yards.'[49] The pattern could be raised again simply by steaming, or the material could be renovated 'by thoroughly brushing all dust from the material, sprinkling with alcohol, and rolling in newspaper, commencing with the paper and the crape together, so that the paper may be between every portion of the material. Allow it to remain so until dry.'[50] Silk, being lighter and less crisp than velvet or crape, was liable to crumple; it could be restored by sponging with 'spirits of wine, diluted with a little water. Then iron it on the wrong side, keeping a piece of muslin between the surface of the silk and the hot iron.'[51] It could also develop shiny patches from continuous friction; these could be removed by 'sponging the glossy part of the silk with some spirit, such as eau de Cologne, ammonia, gin, etc.'[52] Finally if the silk merely needed 'reviving', it could be sponged 'with nearly a dry sponge dipped in a mixture of beer and water and ammonia, in the proportion of a pint of cold water to a teacupfull of stout or porter, in which has been dissolved a lump of salts of ammonia as big as a hazel nut.'[53] It was then to be repeatedly rolled on a roller and shaken until quite dry. '*Do not on any account, use an iron,* and the silk will thus look nearly as good as new.'

The tireless Victorian housewife did not even shrink from water-proofing her own clothes. Calico could be rendered water-resistant by being soaked in water to swell the fibres, wrung dry, and treated with an application of boiled linseed oil. For other fabrics, 'take a pound of glue, and one of tallow bar soap, and dissolve them in five gallons of water. Bring the water to boiling point, and add slowly one and a half pounds of alum. When this is all dissolved, cool the liquid down to 13° Fahr. [*sic*], and, plunging the proposed articles therein, hang them up to dry. When dry they should be washed in soft water and dried a second time. These articles should not be used like ordinary apparel, but only during rain.' [54] Another recipe called for 'one pound of sugar of lead, one pound of alum, one gallon of water; stir all these well together in a pail, let the mixture stand twenty-four hours, pour off the clear water, and be sure to bury the sediment, which is poisonous. Dip the cloth in the liquid, and when thoroughly saturated, take it out and squeeze it well, but do not wring it, as that shrinks the cloth; hang it up to dry, and when nearly so draw the cloth out, fold it, and put it under a heavy weight. This quantity will waterproof five or six yards of wide cloth. I have a cloak which I waterproofed in this way more than five years ago, and it still keeps out the rain perfectly.' [55]

Open fires and candlelight constituted a serious fire hazard, par-ticularly when clothes were long and full and difficult to control (for instance the crinoline skirts of the 'sixties). Accidents were frequent and often serious, so it is not surprising to find numerous recipes for the fireproofing of clothes. 'Half the weight of whitening mixed with the starch will render lace, net, muslin, gauze, or any other light stuff, perfectly uninflammable. As white dresses are much worn at evening parties, where fires are often kept in the grates, and numerous ladies have been burnt to death by means of their dresses catching light whilst dancing, it is hoped this useful receipt will not be forgotten by any lady in the habit of attending balls and parties. This receipt is equally applicable to the lace flounces and other trimmings with which silk dresses are usually adorned.' [56] Equally recommended as fireproof washes were sal ammoniac or phosphate of ammonia, chloride of zinc, alum, or borax and Epsom salts, all in solution. But 'for fabrics which require ironing after washing, tungstate of soda is the only salt which allows the iron to go smoothly over the cloth. The cost is about a penny per dress.'[57]

Notes and References

1   Mary Clive (ed.), *The Diaries and Family Papers of Caroline Clive,* 1949. Entry for 29 April, 1842.

2   *The World of Fashion,* 1841.

3   Ibid., 1849.

4   Ibid., 1853.

5   Mme Carette, *My Mistress, the Empress Eugenie,* quoted in N. Waugh, *The Cut of Women's Clothes,* 1968.

6   Gores are triangular-shaped pieces of material which, when used in a skirt, with the narrowest point at the top, allow fullness at the hem without producing surplus material at the waist.

7   Quoted by Janet Arnold in 'High Victorian', *Costume* (The Journal of the Costume Society), 1968.

8   Quoted in C. W. and P. Cunnington, *Handbook of English Costume in the 19th Century,* 1959. Source unidentified.

9   Ibid.

10   *The Ladies' Treasury,* 1876.

11   Ibid.

12   Quoted by Janet Arnold, op. cit.

13   Quoted in C. W. Cunnington, *English Women's Clothing in the Nineteenth Century,* 1937.

14   Quoted in C. W. and P. Cunnington, op. cit.

15   *The Lady's World,* 1887.

16   Quoted in C. W. Cunnington, op. cit.

17   *The Lady's World,* 1887.

18   *The Woman's World,* 1890.

19   *The Lady's Realm,* 1898-9.

20   Ibid., 1898.

21   Quoted in E. Royston Pike (ed.), *Human Documents of the Victorian Golden Age,* 1969.

22   Quoted in C. W. Cunnington, *The Perfect Lady,* 1948.

23   *The Girl's Own Paper,* 1883.

24   *The Queen,* 1863.

25   Ibid.

26 *Cassell's Household Guide,* Vol. II. Published in four volumes, c. 1868-70.

27 *Miss Leslie's Magazine,* 1843.

28 *Cassell's Household Guide,* Vol. II.

29 *The Englishwoman's Domestic Magazine,* 1879.

30 *The Ladies' Treasury,* 1877.

31 *Miss Leslie's Magazine,* 1843.

32 *Enquire Within,* 1891.

33 *Miss Leslie's Magazine,* 1843.

34 Hippolyte Taine, *Notes on England 1860-70,* 1957 edition.

35 *Home Notes,* 1894.

36 *The Queen,* 1890.

37 Ibid.

38 *The Ladies' Treasury,* 1873.

39 *Enquire Within,* 1893.

40 *The Queen,* 1868.

41 *Enquire Within,* 1894.

42 *The Girl's Own Paper,* 1883.

43 *Enquire Within,* 1894.

44 Ibid.

45 *The Englishwoman's Domestic Magazine,* 1879.

46 *Enquire Within,* 1892.

47 Ibid., 1893.

48 *Cassell's Household Guide,* Vol. II.

49 Viscountess Ridley (ed.), *The Letters of Cecilia Ridley,* 1958.

50 *Enquire Within,* 1892.

51 *The Queen,* 1863.

52 Ibid., 1871.

53 *Cassell's Household Guide,* Vol. II.

54 *The Ladies' Treasury,* 1861.

55 *The Queen,* 1870.

56 *Cassell's Household Guide,* Vol. III.

57 *The Ladies' Treasury,* 1861.

2

Underwear

The Victorians wore far more underwear than we do today, the women, in particular, piling on layer upon layer in the form of assorted bodices and petticoats. This was partly for warmth, but the chief reason was to protect their clothing from the body dirt which causes us to wash our dresses, shirts and sweaters so frequently. For women, a third, equally important function of underwear was that it provided the means of converting the natural body to whatever shape was then fashionable.

The chief instrument of this was the corset, which was worn throughout the Victorian period, varying only in its shape and in minor details of its construction. It was made of strips of whalebone or steel, sandwiched between layers of stout fabric, such as twilled cotton or cotton satin, and reinforced with lines of stitching, cording or quilting.

In the early years of the period, when the ideal waist was long and narrow, the shape was achieved by means of a long, one-piece corset supported by shoulder straps, and shaped at bust and hips by means of gussets. This produced an angular silhouette, which was kept rigid by means of a busk, a long slightly curved piece of wood or whalebone, about two or three inches wide, which was inserted into a pocket down the centre front of the corset. The whole thing was then fastened down the back by means of laces strung through metal eyelet holes, and it was the task of a maid or assistant to haul on these laces and squeeze the wearer to the desired shape.

With the huge crinoline skirts and rising waistlines of the 1860s, corsets became shorter and less restricting. They were now made from separate pieces of material, and could follow the contours of the body more closely. Shoulder straps were no longer necessary, and although back lacing still allowed for extra easing and fit, the actual fastening was at the front, by means of metal loops and studs, over a metal busk. The return of the waist and hips in the sheath-like dresses of the mid 1870s meant that corsets extended once again. The busk lengthened, and in the 1880s and early 1890s it curved and widened at the bottom to produce the 'spoon' busk, which held in the stomach as never before. At this time, corsets were so elaborately pieced together, and stiffened with so many lines of stitching, cording and bones, that their construction rivalled any feat of Victorian technology. The result was a smoother curvature than in previous models, and this was rein-forced by steam moulding, a process by which the corset was heavily starched and then steamed into shape on a metal dummy. The bodices of this period were pulled so tightly across the body that the front fastenings of the corset became visible, and in some cases there was a change to back lacing, which could be hidden under a dress with a back closure.

The more complex the corset grew in structure, the more lavish was its decoration. Those of the 'forties and 'fifties were usually white or drab coloured, and purely functional in design, but the vogue for bright colours that came with the discovery of aniline dyes, produced a fashion for scarlet corsets in the 1860s. The 1870s saw the increasing use of braid and trimming, but it was during the last two decades of the century that decorative elements came into their own. Corsets of this period were often made of figured silks and satins, and trimmed with layers of lace threaded with satin ribbon. Colours were startling. Black with red stitching, or red with orange could be found in the 1880s, and acid yellow appeared in the 1890s. A typically gorgeous version of about 1890 was of pale blue silk with yellow stitching, tied with yellow lacings, and trim-med with white lace and a blue satin bow.

It was very difficult to clean a corset, for they were too thick and heavy to wash. *Home Notes,* in 1895, recommended that plain white ones could be 'brushed over with a mixture of soapy water and ammonia', but too great a wetting would probably have affected the stiffening. Certainly, one writer complained that frequent cleaning was apt to spoil the shape. This does not mean, however, that the Victorian woman was any less scrupulous about keeping her corset clean. On the contrary, she firmly believed that 'A soiled corset is strong evidence of carelessness and lamentable want of neatness in the wearer.' [1] In fact, the Victorian corset was far less vulnerable to dirt than a modern foundation garment, for it was never in direct contact with the body. A chemise was always worn underneath, and for most of the period there was a layer of petticoats or some sort of camisole bodice between the corset and the outer clothing. To ensure absolute cleanliness, however, the wearer usually tacked on an artificial lining, or a 'thin calico loose cover',[2] which could be taken off and washed separately.

While the corset moulded the top half of the body, similar sub-structures were needed to create the surprising variety of skirt shapes found in the Victorian period. Layers of petticoats and a small bustle produced the bell-shaped skirt of the first few years, the bustle consisting of a crescent-shaped pad of down, or stiffened frills of cotton, which was tied round the waist with tapes. As skirts grew wider in the 1840s, the horsehair petticoat, or crinoline (from the French *crin* – horsehair), was introduced to give greater stiffening and fullness. In the 1850s this was worn with as many as six or seven linen or cotton petticoats, in an attempt to achieve still greater width, but the result was extremely hot and uncomfortable. It was with great relief then, that, after 1856, women discarded these layers and adopted the cage.

The cage was a straightforward linen or cotton petticoat, in-serted with hoops of whalebone, and it soon adopted the name, as well as the function, of its horsehair predecessor. Improved versions of this crinoline elaborated the structure until it consisted of narrow rows of angled hoops of whalebone, steel, or gutta-percha, held in place by strips of material. As skirts flattened in front in the 1860s, the crinoline frame flattened too, until, with the growing emphasis on fullness at the back, it became a half-crinoline. By the early 1870s, the upper layers of half-hoops had developed into a bustle shape, or alternatively, a bustle made of layers of horsehair frills was worn over the top. Within a few years, the crinoline had disappeared altogether, leaving only the bustle.

During the 1870s, the fullness moved down the skirt, and sub-sided in a train, but at the beginning of the 1880s the bustle was revived once again. At this time, although sometimes made of

Cotton corset cover and
waist petticoat (1896)

horsehair, it was more usually a long, narrow, concertina-like version of the half-crinoline, consisting of a series of curved half-hoops inserted into a strip of material or into the petticoat itself, and the ends drawn towards each other by tapes. The result was a sharp, angular shape, quite unlike the bustle of the previous decade.

By the end of the 1880s, this too, had dwindled, leaving only a small bustle pad, not unlike those of the early Victorian period, and in the 1890s all structures were finally discarded, leaving the skirt to fit closely over the hips.

It was probably impossible to clean the bustle pads or horsehair structures, but bustles were worn over the petticoats and so were largely protected from dirt. The cage crinoline, on the other hand, had the disadvantage that it was worn under the petticoats, and was long enough for the hem to be vulnerable to mud and to the general wear and tear of walking. According to one writer, 'One good crinoline ought to last for the year, providing yourself with a few yards of extra steel to replace those which may get broken, before they work through the covering, and also a loose cover about nine inches deep round the bottom, which saves the edge, and which can be easily taken off and washed.'[3] Those with gutta-percha hoops had the advantage that the hoops could be cleaned too, simply by rubbing with a damp sponge. Nevertheless, it was usual to keep separate crinolines for day and evening wear.

Under her corset, the Victorian woman wore a voluminous chemise, which usually reached well below her knees. In the early years, this was short-sleeved, with a falling flap at the front to fold down over the corset. After 1860, this disappeared in favour of a low, round neckline and a front opening, and the flap was replaced by a separate, waist-length under-bodice, later called a camisole. In the 'forties and 'fifties, chemises were very plain, relying for their quality on the fineness of the fabric, which was often more like muslin, the tiny, hand-sewn stitches, and perhaps a delicate

Horsehair bustle (1872)

frill at the neck, but from the middle of the century decoration became more acceptable, and sleeves and necklines were edged with layers of openwork embroidery.

Considering the narrow waists of the 1840s and 1850s, it seems surprising that women were prepared to wear so voluminous an under-garment, but perhaps the folds of material were necessary to absorb the perspiration, and to allow some circulation of air under the hot, heavy corset. With the cuirasse bodice of the late 1870s, however, it was felt necessary to shape the chemise, and it became sleeveless, shorter, and was seamed at the waist to give a closer fit. In some cases it was discarded altogether and replaced by combinations, but in general the chemise continued to be worn right into the twentieth century. Towards the end of the Victorian period it became far more decorative, and in 1892 we are told that 'The prettiest chemise is cut either round or heart-shaped. A ribbon run in tightens it a little round the shoulders. It is also buttoned on the shoulder. The neck and shoulders are edged with valenciennes [lace] or a light embroidery.'[4]

Drawers were by no means universal in the first part of the period, for the layers of petticoats ensured both warmth and modesty. Those that were worn were long and voluminous, like the chemise, ending well below the knee. At this time they were open down the inside seams, and held together only at the bottom of the leg, and at the waistband, where they usually fastened at the back with buttons and tapes. Again, the early models were very plain, but from the middle of the century the legs were often edged with openwork embroidery.

In the late 1870s, when the chemise began to narrow and shorten, it was often united with drawers to produce a new, all-in-one garment, combinations. Although they never entirely replaced the separate chemise and drawers, combinations were one solution to the need for tighter-fitting underwear. Most were made of cotton, and they became increasingly decorative in the 1880s, with lace or openwork frills, threaded with ribbon, round the neck, sleeves and legs.

Over the chemise, corset, and drawers, came the petticoat. In the early years, many were still full length, consisting of a gathered skirt and a sleeveless bodice with a pointed waist, just like the dress above it. For most of the period, however, the usual form was the waist-petticoat – a petticoat without an attached bodice – and these could be piled one on top of the other to fill out the skirt.

In the 1840s, the fashionable bell-shaped skirt and long narrow waist was achieved by means of very full petticoats gathered onto a deep curved waistband or yoke, which tied or buttoned at the back. Layers of petticoats, starched, and stiffened round the hem with rows of cording, gave extra support to the horsehair crinoline. With the arrival of the hooped crinoline these layers were usually discarded, leaving just one or two cotton petticoats worn over the top, to soften the line of the hoops. These were usually trimmed with tucks and openwork embroidery round the hem.

In the 1870s and 1880s, petticoats again followed the line of the skirt, with tie-back tapes and flounced hems. With the long, tight, cuirasse bodice, the full-length 'princess' style was revived to give a smooth, unbroken line. Alternatively, waist-petticoats could be worn under the corset, arranged on a shaped band to avoid any unnecessary bulk. The more *avant-garde* left off petticoats altogether, keeping only some extra flounces inside the hem of the skirt and a separate petticoat train attached at the back. By the end of the century, petticoats had become very elaborate, fitted at the top to allow the gored skirts to cling round the hips, and with layers of embroidered and lace-edged flounces at the hem.

Linen and cotton were the chief fabrics used for underwear, but from the 1880s wools and silks became increasingly popular. Flannel underwear had long been used for warmth in really cold weather. In 1849 Effie Ruskin had written, 'The approaching winter seems to have begun severely and in addition to the flannel drawers I got before I left Scotland I have now added flannel chemises, and I do not think I shall find them a bit too warm.'[5] During the 1860s, bright red flannel petticoats were fashionable, but it was during the 1880s that wool really came into its own for all types of underwear. This was due largely to the work of a German professor, Dr Gustav Jaeger. He criticized silk and vegetable fibres, and claimed that wool, being more absorbent, could cure all sorts of ills by preventing the retention of the 'noxious exhalations' of the body. He recommended fitted clothes such as long drawers and combinations in undyed knitted wools, and from 1884 such garments were manufactured in England, bearing the label 'Dr. Jaeger's Sanitary Wool System'. Jaeger soon modified his ideas on colour, however, and both natural wool and red flannel became favourite materials for underwear and nightwear, to the end of the

LADIES' UNDERCLOTHING
Direct from Manufacturer, saving fully 25 per cent.

Night Dress, "Sterling," trim'd fine work, prettily tucked, pure cloth 3/-.

Nt. Dress, "Hibernia," by Irish Peasants, various designs, from 4 6 to 2½/-

Chemise, trimmed Swiss work, "Sterling," in pretty designs, 3 6.

The New "Alpine" Natural Wool Combinations, 7-, 8 6, 10 6, 12 6. Slip Bodices, 3 6 and 4 6.

Knickers, "Sterling,"double frill, rich work, 3/-.

Knickers, "Sterling," fine Swiss work, good cloth, 2 -.

Ch'dren's "Sterling Chemises, 1st size - 10¼, 8 larger sizes.

Ch'dren's "Sterling"N't Dresses, 1st size, 1/9, 8 larger sizes.

BABY LINEN DEPARTMENT.—Employs over One Hundred Needlewomen.

CHRISTENING ROBES.	CASHMERE CLOAKS.	SILK & SATIN HATS & HOODS.
Robes fully Trimmed, 5/- to 25/-. Robes Handsomely trimmed, 21/- to 10 Guineas.	Braided or Embroidered, 7/6 to 42/-. Special Designs, 21/- to 10 guineas.	Hats and Hoods, Silk or Cashmere, 3/6 to 15 6. Handsome Designs, 7/6 to 50/-.

Catalogues and Illustrated Sheets of 50 engravings post free of

R. ALLIN, 73 & 78, Upper St., & 464, Kingsland Rd., London. Stock Valuations made. 20 years' experience.

Demy 8vo., Cloth Boards, Price 4s. 6d.

TRAVELS IN VARIOUS PARTS OF EUROPE,
During the Years 1888, 1889, and 1890.
Being a Short and Practical Account. By GILBERT H. W. HARRISON.
WITH 24 ILLUSTRATIONS.

"Mr. Harrison's notes about Dresden, Budapest, Leipzig, and the old Spanish and Portuguese towns have only one failing—they are too short."—*Publishers' Circular.*

"A short and practical account, which the tourist will find of service. . . Quite a mine of information on things Continental."—*Scottish Leader.*

"Should prove of considerable value to those about to visit any of the places referred to in the book, and in doubt as to an eligible place for their next tour."—*Lakes Herald.*

"Has the merit of containing, within very small compass, a graphic account of some of the most striking scenery to be met with in a large part of Europe."—*Morning Advertiser.*

LONDON: BEMROSE AND SONS, 23, OLD BAILEY; AND DERBY.

THE "DUCHESS" CORSET
(THOMAS'S PATENT)

Is constructed on a graceful model for the present style of dress, the shape being permanently retained by a series of narrow whalebones placed diagonally across the front, gradually curving in and contracting the Corset at the bottom of the busk, whereby the size of the figure is reduced, the outline improved, a permanent support afforded, and a fashionable and elegant appearance secured.

The Corsets are Black, White, Cardinal, Dove, and Grey.

The Celebrated Patent TAPER BUSK used is THE MOST SUPPLE and COMFORTABLE of ALL BUSKS, and QUITE UNBREAKABLE.

Inferior imitations of the Duchess Corset are numberless, rendering it necessary to see that the name "W. Thomas" is stamped inside of Corset.

OF ALL DRAPERS AND OUTFITTERS.

Sole Proprietors of THOMAS'S PATENT DUCHESS CORSET—WHOLESALE ONLY—

YOUNG, CARTER, AND OVERALL,
117 & 118, WOOD STREET, LONDON,
To whom please write for address of nearest Retailer, if any difficulty in procuring.

Advertisements for underwear from *The Ladies' Treasury*

century.

Victorian nightwear was closely related to the daytime underwear. For most of the period women wore nightcaps, and ankle-
length nightgowns which were very similar to the chemise, except
that they had long sleeves and high necks. Like the chemise, the
nightgowns of the early years were of white linen, their sole decoration a frill at the neck and wrists, but after the middle of the century cotton came into more general use and tucks and openwork
embroidery became a feature. The appearance of combinations in
the 1870s had some influence on nightwear, for in 1886 there was
an advertisement for 'The combination nightgown or lady's
pyjama', a confection which required four and a half yards of
calico or flannel, and was made as an all-in-one garment with frills
at the knees and wrists. Pyjamas did not become generally popular
for women until the 1920s, however, and nightgowns of linen,
cotton or flannel continued in general wear for the rest of the
period. They too became more elaborate in the last two decades of
the nineteenth century. 'The night chemise should reach down to
the feet and have long sleeves. It is trimmed with frills, embroideries, or lace, and is finished off with a large collar, falling to the
shoulders in pleats. Ribbons are sometimes put in at the collar and
cuffs. It is, of course, made of washing material.'[6]

Men's underwear consisted of a vest and a pair of long drawers
of some stout material. 'For men, drawers are composed of very
strong twill calico, linen, flannel and stockinet.'[7] These changed
little in style, although in the 1880s woollen combinations became
popular, and flannel was much used for vests and drawers. In the
early part of the century, men's nightwear consisted of a nightgown very similar to that worn by women, and a conical nightcap
of wool or knitted silk. These could be plain or striped, and sometimes had ear flaps, but, like women's nightcaps, they ceased to be
fashionable towards the end of the century. The gown was generally discarded with the cap, to be replaced by the new 'pyjama
sleeping suit'.

Notes and References

1 Baroness Staffa, *The Lady's Dressing-Room,* 1892.
2 *How To Dress Well on A Shilling A Day,* by Sylvia, c. 1873.
3 *How To Dress on £15 a Year, as a Lady,* by a Lady, 1873.
4 *The Lady's Dressing-Room,* op. cit.
5 Mary Lutyens (ed.), *Effie in Venice, Edited Letters of Mrs. John Ruskin 1849-52,* 1965.
6 *The Lady's Dressing-Room,* op. cit.
7 *The Workwoman's Guide,* by a Lady, 1838.

3
Washing

❖

Nowadays almost all our clothing can be cleaned in the family washing machine. Heavy or delicate fabrics go to the dry-cleaners, and only fine knitted woollens and the most delicate garments require special attention. For the Victorians, however, cleaning presented a far greater problem, for the variety and delicacy of their fabrics, and the dubious quality of their dyes, meant that a whole range of clothes such as silk dresses, lace collars, heavy foundation garments, and coloured cottons, all required special methods of cleaning. Straightforward washing with soap and hot water was reserved chiefly for the plain white cottons and linens. However, as these included the underwear and nightwear for the whole household, together with the children's dresses and baby-wear; men's shirts; pinafores and aprons, collars and cuffs; and all the domestic linen, there was still plenty to wash in the normal manner. (A list of the typical garments included in a family wash of 1838 may be found on page 57.)

Wash-day took place far less frequently than nowadays, but not because the Victorians were any less clean. On the contrary, of their many layers of underclothes only the bottommost layer was subject to body dirt, and those items were changed frequently. We are told that a woman with good taste 'prefers comparatively simple underlinen, which there is no fear of washing, and which can be changed daily.'[1] Some magazines even advocated that she should change her underwear every time she changed from morning to afternoon dress. The washing was done infrequently for the

simple reason that it involved a great deal of mess and upheaval
in the household, and that it was both more convenient and more
economical to save up the dirty linens and wash a large number of
items at one time. In 1838, *The Workwoman's Guide* recommended: 'It is the best economy to wash by the year, or by the
quarter, in places where it can be done, and by the score or dozen
in preference to the piece.' From this, the practice of infrequent
washing became a status symbol, for only well-to-do families could
afford sufficient clothing to make it possible. In the 1890s, Miss
Lane, the postmistress of Candleford Green, 'still kept to the old
middle-class country custom of one huge washing of linen every
six weeks. In her girlhood it would have been thought poor looking
to have had a weekly or fortnightly washday. The better off a
family was, the more changes of linen its members were supposed
to possess.'[2] Thus, for most of the nineteenth century, the weekly
wash was the preserve of the poorer households, where no one was
likely to own more than 'three of everything'. For most middle-
class families, the wash was usually fortnightly at least.

In a house with children and servants, a fortnightly wash could
involve several hundred items, and washing, drying and ironing
had to be spread over several days, for there were few labour-
saving devices to speed up the process. Washing machines were
available in the nineteenth century, but they were not very
efficient. These early models usually consisted of a wooden tub or
box on legs which rocked or rotated in order to circulate the
clothes. Many manufacturers tried to reproduce the action of
hand-rubbing by lining the tub with wooden spikes or ridges. The
popular 'Bradford's Vowel' was corrugated at the bottom 'by
means of wooden bars studded with what look like large, smooth
wooden buttons, against which the linen rubs as the barrel is
turned.'[3] In another version, 'the clothes are worked backwards
and forwards between two rollers.'[4]

Unfortunately, these techniques were too harsh for delicate
fabrics, and some were said to 'wrench off buttons and wear out
linen.'[5] They were also accused of being heavy on soap. Another
disadvantage was that, before the advent of mains electricity, these
machines had to be operated by hand, and they were so heavy and
cumbersome that many servants refused to use them. It was not
until the latter half of the century that these problems were overcome by machines such as the 'Torpedo'. This was 'a cigar-shaped

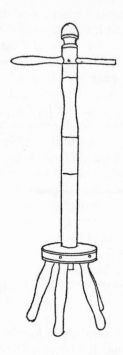

A washing dolly

affair . . . which possessed neither teeth, nor spokes, nor spikes, nor ridges.' Made of corrugated iron, it was constructed 'like two wine-glasses hermetically sealed together'. The inside was perfectly smooth, and the whole thing was operated by steam. 'It washes one hundred articles more easily than fifty, for it is a question of balance with the "Torpedo", a balance so perfect when well packed with clothes, that a slight tap of the laundrymaid's hand is sufficient to keep it in motion.' Unfortunately, however, these wonder machines often provoked deep suspicion, and even this writer had to admit that 'many of my servants do not approve of "them new-fangled notions", so the laundry is furnished plenti-fully with other ways of washing.'[6] So much for the machine age.

For most of the century, washing was done by hand in large oaken or earthenware tubs, and the only concessions to mechanical washing techniques were the 'washing dolly', a three- or four-legged pole for pounding and rotating especially tough and dirty linens, and the 'peggy tub', whose corrugated interior was used to the same purpose.

Many households were also prepared to invest in a mangle for pressing the dry, heavy linens, and, later in the century, smaller wringers could be bought which attached to the side of the washing tub and were used to squeeze the water out of the wet clothes. In the second half of the nineteenth century they were still a novelty in many areas. D. H. Lawrence, in *The Rainbow*, describes Anna's reaction to being given just such a wringer by her father. ' "How does it go?" she asked. "Why it's for pulpin' turnips," he replied. She looked at him. His voice disturbed her. "Don't be silly. It's a little mangle," she said. "How do you stand it, though?" "You screw it on the side o' your wash-tub." ' A few minutes later her father finds her in the scullery 'with the little wringer fixed on the dolly-tub, turning blissfully at the handle, and Tilly beside her, exclaiming "My word, that's a natty little thing! That'll save you lugging your inside out. That's the latest contraption, that is. . . . It fair runs by itself. . . . Your clothes'll nip out on to the line." ' [7]

It was not long before adjustable wringers could be adapted for both wringing and mangling, and by 1880, according to *The Girl's Own Paper*, 'The little inexpensive wringing machines, which press out moisture and serve also as mangles, may be found in the possession of most cottage laundresses, especially those who "take in washing". In large cities, a person in a poor neighbourhood will make a living by such a machine, a trifle being paid per dozen for wringing large things, and again for mangling.'

Even with the help of these early labour-saving devices, washday still involved much lifting of wet and heavy clothes from tub to tub, through the various stages of soaping and rinsing, and much refilling of tubs and emptying of dirty water. It was thus a very wet and messy business, and those involved took good care to wear suitable protective clothing. Miss Bond wore a large heavy apron and special cuffs, while Mrs Bowen appeared attired in 'a huge holland overall that draped her from throat to wrist and from neck to hem.' [8] To protect their feet from the sodden floor many women put on the traditional country overshoes called pattens, by which the feet were raised up on a metal ring. Nothing, however, could protect them from the heat and steam, or prevent the coarsening of their hands after hour upon hour immersed in hot water, soap, soda and ammonia.

Not surprisingly, those who could afford such a luxury sent their washing out to a laundress. Laura was much impressed by the 'solid comfort' of her aunt's house, where 'instead of the damp and steam of washday, . . . a woman came every Monday morning and carried the week's washing away,' bringing it back clean at the end of the week.[9] The system was not without its serious disadvantages, however. One writer in *The Girl's Own Paper* of 1889 was used to sending all her dirty linens to a 'decent body' nearby, but 'Alas! With a certain basket of well-starched linen came, one day, to No. 32, particularly terrible microbes and spores and germs. Mrs Fowler [the decent body] had scarlet fever in her country cottage.' This was a common occurrence, and such diseases were often spread by laundry-women. Even influenza could be carried from house to house in the clothes-basket.

In small households, where the washing *was* done at home, usually by the maid and the mistress, it could involve considerable upset for the whole family, for then wash-day meant that there would be no one to carry out the daily tasks of cleaning, preparing meals and the like. *The Girl's Own Paper* advised that on such a day the whole family should get up early so that the maid might fit in two hours' work before breakfast, while 'the preparation of the meal might be made much easier if her mistress were an early riser on that day, for the eggs might be boiled and the tea made in the dining-room, and the breakfast things cleared away and washed up, even by herself.'[10] Better still, the day before wash-day, the mistress of the house could have arranged a cold joint of beef, some pickles, and a cold pudding, so that the maid did not have to stop and prepare a midday meal, and, hopefully, she would have finished the washing 'ready to change and lay the table for late dinner.'

The degree of upheaval depended largely on where the washing was to take place. In a good-sized country house there was usually a separate wash-house, bleaching house, and ironing and drying room, and sometimes even a special drying closet, heated by a furnace. Such wash-houses were specially fitted out with sloping brick floors to allow the water to run away into the drain, and some were plumbed to supply hot and cold water direct to the washing tubs. In town houses, the washing was usually done below stairs, in the basement, and here too there was often a direct water

462 **HARROD'S STORES, Limited, Brompton.**
IRONMONGERY AND TURNERY.
No. 10 DEPARTMENT—*FIRST FLOOR.*

WRINGING MACHINES—*continued.*

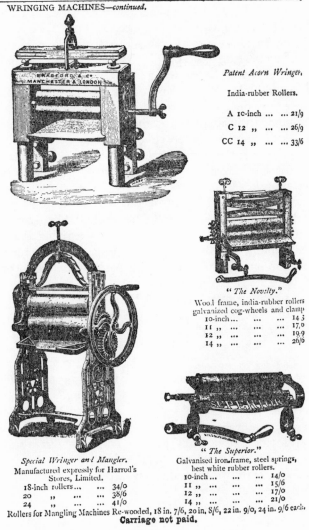

Patent Acorn Wringer,

India-rubber Rollers.

A 10-inch 21/9
C 12 ,, ... 26/9
CC 14 ,, ... 33/6

"The Novelty."
Wool frame, india-rubber rollers
galvanized cog-wheels and clamp
10-inch... ... ... 14 3
11 ,, ... 17,0
12 ,, ... 19,9
14 ,, ... 26/6

Special Wringer and Mangler.
Manufactured expressly for Harrod's
Stores, Limited.
18-inch rollers... ... 34/0
20 ,, ... 38/6
24 ,, ... 41/0

"The Superior."
Galvanised iron-frame, steel springs,
best white rubber rollers.
10-inch... ... ... 14/0
11 ,, ... 15/6
12 ,, ... 17/0
14 ,, ... 21/0

Rollers for Mangling Machines Re-wooded, 18 in. 7/6, 20 in, 8/6, 22 in. 9/0, 24 in. 9/6 each.
Carriage not paid.

Mangles, from Harrod's Catalogue, 1895

supply; indeed it was often the only part of the house to have running water. Many country cottages would have a small, lean-to wash-house where the water was heated by a copper, so the washing was still separated from the living area, but in really small houses, of 'two up, two down' or less, the only place for washing might be 'in the one room that serves for parlour, kitchen, and every purpose, except sleeping.'[11] There, water would have to be heated in pots over the fire, and all the soaping, rinsing, ironing and airing would take place in the one room. No wonder then, that the family complained of 'the domestic misery and discomfort which accompanied washing day . . . the scolding wife, the truant husband, crying and neglected children, meals ill prepared, or not prepared at all; the sloppy kitchen, deserted by the cat; and the favourite dog kicked out of doors, and not daring to show his honest muzzle.'[12]

Those small establishments who could afford to do so, usually brought in a hired help. 'For the big wash at Miss Lane's, a professional washerwoman came for two days, arriving at six o'clock on the Monday morning, in a clean apron and sun-bonnet, with a second apron of sacking and a pair of pattens in a large open basket upon her arm.'[13] Earlier in the century, or in very large establishments, washerwomen were paid by the piece (see page 57) but Miss Lane's woman was paid by the day. For two days' work she earned three shillings, plus her food and something to take away in her basket. This seems to have been the usual sort of rate, for *Cassell's Household Guide,* in the late 1860s, quoted the average pay of washerwomen in and around London as two shillings per day 'provided food and beer be found, and half-a-crown if required to "find herself".'

In many cases, however, the 'help' was little more than a child, and was paid substantially less. In Dickens's *Bleak House,* the thirteen-year-old orphan girl, 'Charley', when asked how she keeps herself and her brothers and sisters, replies: ' "Since father died, Sir, I've gone out to work. I'm out washing today." "God help you, Charley. You're not tall enough to reach the tub." "In pattens I am, Sir," she said quickly. "I've got a high pair as belonged to mother." "And do you often go out?" "As often as I can," said Charley, opening her eyes, and smiling, "because of earning sixpences and shillings." '[14]

The hired help was expected to undertake only the actual wash-

LADY'S WASHING BOOK.

Number.	Number.		Price.	£.	s.	d.
		Aprons	½			
		Caps, Bonnet	1			
		—— Night	1			
		Collars	1			
		Dresses	4d. or 6d.			
		Dressing Gowns................................	3			
		Flannel ditto	3			
		Drawers	1			
		Flannel Petticoats	1			
		Flannel Drawers	2			
		Flannel Waistcoats	1			
		Frills	1			
		Habit Shirts	½			
		Jackets	2			
		Night Gowns	2			
		Neck Handkerchiefs	½			
		Pocket ditto	½			
		Napkins	½			
		Pockets	½			
		Petticoats	2			
		Socks, pairs of	1			
		Stockings, pairs of	1			
		Shifts	2			
		Stays	6			
		Skirts	2			
		Shawls	2			
		Tippets	1			

A lady's laundry list

ing; the preparation of clothes and wash-house, and the business of mangling, ironing, airing, etc., were done by the servant and the ladies of the house. The actual washing was only part of the whole business, which usually lasted several days. Thus *The Girl's Own Paper* of 1899 recommended the following programme for a fortnightly wash: 'Steeping on Monday; washing on Tuesday; folding and starching on Wednesday; ironing on Thursday; airing on Friday.' In many cases, the clothes were prepared on Saturday, so that the washing proper could begin on Monday morning, but this had the disadvantage that 'in hot weather especially, the water is apt to smell badly if dirty clothes lie in it from Saturday to Monday.'[15] The full preparation involved collecting all the dirty items from where they had been stored, usually in a special box or a bin in the housemaid's closet; removing all the stains, by a whole variety of methods (see Chapter 10); separating the woollens and printed fabrics; and dividing the rest into delicate garments, ordinary linen, and especially dirty household linens, such as towels, dish cloths, greasy aprons, etc. These were then put to soak, with a little extra rub for soiled collars and cuffs and some soda with the greasy items.

On wash-day itself the maid got up especially early in order to prepare the hot water and the equipment for washing. In most households the water was heated, and the clothes boiled, in a copper, which, 'If required for large washings . . . should be capable of holding eighteen or twenty gallons of water.'[16] (On other occasions it was used for brewing beer.) Having filled this, and lit the fire underneath it, she then dusted the tubs, wringer, mangle and clothes-line, together with the wicker baskets used for carrying the clothes out to the line. She then prepared the soap. This was usually the yellow household variety, although white curd soap was sometimes used on more delicate garments. It was bought in lumps, by the stone or the ton in large households, and cut into bars with a piece of wire like a cheese-cutter. It was usually kept stacked in a pyramid on top of a shelf or cupboard, so that the air could circulate round it and dry it out, thus making it harder and more concentrated. Soap could be rubbed directly onto particularly soiled or greasy areas, but in most cases it was cut up and dissolved in boiling water to form a semi-liquid soap jelly. When this, in turn, was added to the tubs of hot water, it mixed in easily and produced an even, strong, soapy solution in which to immerse the clothes.

There were alternatives to soap, however. Paraffin was used as an early form of detergent, both when soaking the clothes and when boiling them in the copper, and it was found to be an excellent solvent for grease, provided that sufficient soap and water was mixed with it to prevent the formation of a scum. Another good, and cheap, substitute for soap was the soapwort plant, whose leaves and flowers produce a large quantity of alkali when boiled in water.

When everything was ready, the washerwoman, with the aid of the servant, launched in on the actual washing.

The major part of the wash was devoted to the white linens and cottons, for which there was a strict programme. 'There are three operations in washing – soaking, scrubbing, and boiling; and the order of these should never be changed, nor must the house-

mistress ever permit the boiling to precede the scrubbing for the clothes should be clean before being put into the copper.'[17] Otherwise the dirt could set permanently into the fabric. Firstly then, the clothes were taken out of soak and each garment squeezed through the wringer. They were then transferred to another tub filled with hot soapy water, and squeezed and kneaded to release the dirt without putting too much wear on the fabric. Only collars and cuffs and stubborn stains were rubbed with extra soap. Each item was then passed through the wringer yet again, and transferred to another tub of clean warm rinsing water. After a third wringing, they were ready to be boiled, and were lifted into the copper which had been half filled with hot soapy water. They were then simmered from anything from half an hour to a whole afternoon. Finer, more delicate garments were tied up in a calico bag before being put in the copper, to protect them from the action of the water. Where no copper was available, the clothes were boiled up in the family cooking pots, over the fire, and a real trial it must have been for often 'these inadequate vessels would boil over and fill the house with ashes and steam.'[18]

After boiling, the clothes were well rinsed: 'the first rinsing after the boiling should be in clear, clean hot water, the second in cooler, and last in cold water, plenty of water being needed.'[19] As can be imagined, with so large a wash and the constant filling and empty- ing of the washing tubs, it was only too easy to leave particles of soap and soda or other cleaning agents in the fabrics, and these eventually turned the garments yellow. To improve the colour it was usual to blue the final rinsing water, which had the effect of turning the yellow to a more acceptable grey-white. 'The blue is tied up in a piece of stout linen, and the water is coloured by draw- ing the bag thus made in and out through the water, till it is well mixed and of a suitable colour. . . . All blueing water should be very well mixed, for if not it may cause streaks in the linen.'[20] Similarly, 'Too much blue is a great mistake. It looks ugly by daylight, and by gaslight [which was very yellow] gives, what should be white articles, a grey appearance.'[21]

To make linens really white, bleaches and water-softeners were added to the washing water. 'To make a good washing prepara- tion, put one pound of saltpetre into a gallon of water, and keep it in a corked jug; two tablespoonfuls for a pint of soap. Soap, wash, and boil as usual. This bleaches the clothes beautifully, without injuring the fabric.'[22] Borax was a popular alternative. 'There is nothing like borax for whitening clothes, besides which it is cheap and does not rot the linen like many other bleaching preparations do. It is used by dissolving it in boiling water. Use one tablespoon- ful of borax to every pailful of water. Pour the borax water over the things after they have been washed, and let them stand for some hours; then boil or not as liked. Many laundresses do not boil linen after using the borax water, as they think this whitens them sufficiently.'[23] In fact, borax is not a bleach, but a water-softener less alkali than soda, and so did not yellow the clothes after repeated washes. Another, more unusual method was recom- mended in *The Ladies' Treasury* of 1872: 'Take four pounds of potatoes; scrape or thinly peel and wash them; boil them till three parts done.' The linens, after being steeped in cold water and

Outdoor dresses, 1859. Huge crinoline skirts are exaggerated by flounces, trimmings and
lace shawls.

5 Ball dresses, 1862. Flounces, flowers and lace ornament both dress and hair. (*Le Monde Elegant*)

4 Day dresses, 1862. Jaunty hats rival bonnets above still wider crinolines. (*Le Monde Elegant*)

boiled, were then rubbed with the potatoes in the same manner as with soap. 'After the linen has been well rubbed and wrung, replace it in the boiler with whatever remains of the potatoes; then boil for half an hour.' After the linen had been taken out and again rubbed, wrung out, and returned to the copper, it was finally rinsed two or three times in soft water, steeped for another half hour in cold water, wrung again and then hung out on a line to dry. 'The whole operation does not take more than two and a half hours. The linen thus bleached is perfectly white without the least trace of grease or stains. Kitchen cloths, however greasy, become perfectly clean, and quite inodourous by this process.'

One of the best ways of bleaching whites was, of course, to hang them out in the fresh air and sunshine, as oxygen acts as a natural bleach in the presence of moisture and light. 'There is no surer way to bleach linen that is yellow or discoloured than to pass it through several waters, and hang it to dry in the sun where it is very hot. When dry, wet again, and hang out once more. Repeat as many times as necessary until the linen is bleached.' [24] Sunshine was not essential, however, for in winter an equally efficient method was to soak the linens and 'put them out for a night or two when frosty. They will be nicely bleached when washed.' [25]

So much for cottons and linens, but woollens formed quite a large proportion of the family wash, especially at the end of the century. They were much more difficult to wash as both hot water and the alkalis in soap and water softeners caused them to shrink and yellow, while rubbing, wringing, or over-handling made the fibres felt together. Garments were easily ruined by bad washing, as when Mrs Bowen sent her Jaeger flannels out to a laundress. 'Those articles had been so soft and flexible when they went away. They had returned shrunk up and hard, almost as a millboard. Emmie's combinations were only just fit for Anne, the second girl, while Mr Bowen's vests were diminished woefully.' [26]

The successful washing of woollen fabrics depended on speed. 'Do not on any account begin washing flannels unless you are certain to finish them, as they cannot remain in soak, the least stoppage in the process of washing them will spoil them completely.' [27] Instead, without any prior soaking, they were plunged straight into the washing solution, the most popular recipe being a mixture of soapy water and ammonia (a tablespoonful of ammonia to two gallons of water). The ammonia bleached the wool, without the harsh effects of soda. It was also essential to ensure that the water was not too hot. *The Girl's Own Paper* of 1892 advised checking the temperature with a thermometer, 94°F being the necessary heat for the washing and all the rinsing waters. Once in the washing tub, the woollens were usually washed by drawing them up and down and 'working them about without rubbing or using more soap',[28] but Mrs Bowen was shown a different method by which they *could* be left to soak for an hour, provided that the tub be covered by a lid – a pastry board would do – to prevent any evaporation, and to ensure that the clothes remained completely immersed. After this, they ought to be completely clean, but any stubborn stains, or marks on collars and cuffs, could be rubbed very gently.

After the clothes had been squeezed out, or passed through an adjustable rubber wringer, well rinsed two or three times, and wrung out again, they were given a good shake and hung to dry. This could be done either outside on a line, or on a clothes-horse or 'maiden' indoors. In the latter case it was essential to ensure that they were not in direct heat; if they began to steam vigorously, then they were too hot, and would soon shrink.

The soap and ammonia were usually sufficient to whiten flannels, but they could be blued to counteract any yellowing. In fact, *Cassell's Household Guide* advised that 'It is not possible to blue it [flannel] too much, for new flannel, it will be observed, is very blue; and it is the liberal blueing of flannel which keeps it a good colour.' Alternatively, 'suspending in sulphur fumes is good for all white woollen articles. It prevents their shrinking and getting discoloured and yellow. A common barrel, which can stand on a piece of metal or flat stone, or an old tin pan, to hold the live coals and sulphur; two or three sticks on the top of the barrel, on which to hang the articles to be bleached, and a blanket or an old rug, to cover over all; are the sole articles needed for the bleaching process.'[29]

Coloured flannels, like the bright red petticoats, were washed separately, and it was important to clean them without fading or streaking the colours with over-strong cleaning agents. *Enquire Within*, of 1894, recommended soft rain water, with a dash of ammonia, and then drying the flannel quickly in a wind, but *Home Notes* recommended the following: 'Stir two tablespoons of flour into one quart of cold water. Let it boil ten minutes, add warm suds and wash the flannel in this, using the hands instead of the wash-ing-board. Rinse in three waters, all of the same temperature. Even bright scarlet flannel will never lose its colour when once treated.' [30]

Clothes were best dried outside, for the sake of both the garments and the comfort of the family. Many country folk still followed the old practice of laying out the washing on the grass, or draping it over a hedge, but it was usually hung on lines, placed according to the nature of the garment, so that while 'sheets and pillow-cases and towels were billowing in the wind on a line the whole length of the garden, Miss Lane's more intimate personal wear dried modestly on a line by the hen house, out of the men's sight.' [31] The washing was hung out even in the snow. 'Faint with fatigue, and with every pore opened by the steam from the boiling suds, women go and hang out the clothes, perhaps standing in snow and slush until their feet are numb.' [32] The alternative, however, when it rained, and all the clothes had to be dried indoors, draped on clothes-horses or airers, was far more unpleasant. According to Flora Thompson, 'no-one who has not experienced it can imagine the misery of living for several days with a firmament of drying clothes on lines overhead.' [33] To describe someone disagreeable as 'about as pleasant as a wet wash-day' had far more force then than it does now.

As with all the difficulties of washing, it was in the small crowded city houses that the problem of drying was most acute. Ruth Lamb, in *The Girl's Own Paper* of 1880, investigated the various methods of drying clothes used in urban districts:

'The drying of clothes in close city neighbourhoods is a great difficulty, and, in small streets with little traffic, is often done on lines stretched across the street itself. . . .

'The very queerest mode of drying I ever saw, though, and the strangest collection of duds, were in Edinburgh. It was on a Satur-day afternoon, the washing day of the locality – the closest of closes in the auld toun. The pieces of garments – for there was not a whole one amongst them – were fastened to sticks and hung from the windows, story above story.

'Our driver said that, in all probability, the adult male owners were in bed whilst the fragments were being washed, and the child-ren ditto, unless the younger mortals were too restless, in which case they were probably careering up and down in, let us say, the primeval costume of the Garden of Eden.'

After the linens and woollens had all been washed and put to dry, the work was still not over: 'the last business is to scrub and clean all the utensils, clear out the copper, and tidy the cellar or washhouse. Let us hope some thoughtful little girl has the tea ready, so that there may be a refreshing cup for mother.'[34] She must certainly have needed one!

So much for the actual washing of the clothes, which usually took only one day. The next day was devoted to folding and starching. The men's shirts were the chief articles to be starched (see Chapter 8), but 'The use of extremely thin water starch for all white under-clothing, makes it easier to wash and to keep a good colour, besides improving the appearance.'[35] This starch was made by diluting thick boiled starch until it was almost as thin as water. Frills, caps and aprons were also stiffened, usually by mixing one tablespoonful of white starch and half a small teaspoonful of melted borax in two tablespoonfuls of cold water. To this was added some candle wax, and the mixture simmered and stirred until it became a transparent jelly. The frills, etc. were then dipped in this mixture while it was still hot. The cold-starched items could be ironed straightaway, while they were still wet, but those which had been hot-starched had to be dried first, or else the iron would stick to the starch.

Having been dried on the line or on the clothes-horse, clothes had to be dampened again before being ironed or mangled. The mangle was used chiefly for heavy linens such as sheets and towels, rather than for clothes, for it was liable to break buttons and crush pleats and frills, but woollens were sometimes mangled and given a good shake as an alternative to being ironed on the wrong side.

In the Victorian household, ironing was as complicated a process as washing, and involved just as much equipment. Different garments required different types of iron and, of course, all the irons had to be heated by external means; in addition, since the heat could not be maintained for long, for every iron in use there had to be several more being heated up.

The basic iron was the flat-iron, which was heated on the stove or in front of the fire. Made entirely of metal, it could become extremely hot, even red-hot, and since there were no insulated handles, it could only be picked up with the aid of a padded holder. An experienced laundress could gauge the correct temperature for

HEBDEN'S
SILVER GLOSS
FOR LINEN.
Cheaper and better than Starch Gloss Powders,
and gives a dazzling smoothness to the fabric.
Sold everywhere in Blocks, at 3d. and 6d. each.
Samples post paid on receipt of stamps
value of size wanted.
In writing mention this paper.
W. C. HEBDEN, Albany Works, HALIFAX.

Ironing collars

the garment by holding the iron near her cheek or by spitting on it, but it was safer to try it out on a sample piece of fabric first, rather than risk scorching the garment. The other great disadvantage of flat-irons was that they became smoky and sooty from the fire, and this, with the clinging residue of starch from the clothes, meant that they had to be cleaned constantly. The starch could be removed from the irons by washing them with kerosene, or with soapy water and ammonia. Otherwise they were wiped with sandpaper or coarse salt, or rubbed on a board sprinkled with bathbrick, and then polished with a duster. Used properly, however, they were extremely efficient on large, plain areas of fabric, such as petticoats, and the bodies of shirts, nightgowns and chemises.

According to Ruth Lamb, in 1880, 'Box-irons are less used than they once were,'[36] but they were preferable to flat-irons for more delicate garments. Being hollow, and heated by pieces of red-hot metal placed inside them, they remained cooler and cleaner than flat-irons, and were thus less liable to mark or scorch dainty collars and cuffs. They were still quite difficult to use, however, as the metal had to be inserted by means of tongs. If insufficiently hot, it would not heat the iron, but, if it had been heated for too long, the metal expanded and would not fit inside.

Other methods of internal heating were explored in the charcoal-iron and the spirit-iron, but the former was said to give off soot, and the latter was highly inflammable.

The ironing of flat areas of fabric was usually done on an ironing board or a 'clean deal table,'[37] but it was quite usual to have a range of boards of different shapes – a rectangular one for shirt fronts, a wedge-shaped one for skirts and petticoats, and a long, narrow one for sleeves.

The rows of delicate frills, which were the chief decoration on nightgowns, aprons, chemises and caps, required special 'goffering' or 'gauffering' irons. For large frills, an Italian iron was used. This was a long, hollow, cigar-shaped piece of metal, fixed to a stand. A smaller piece of red-hot metal was inserted inside it, on the same principle as the box-iron, and then a section of the fabric was wrapped tightly round it, until it retained the tubular shape. Tiny fluted frills could be produced by pressing the fabric onto a fluted wooden crimping board with a type of fluted rolling pin. Other methods included wrapping the frill around tongs, or a blunt knife, or laying the fabric alternatively over and under a line of straws.

Altogether, the business of washing and ironing was long, complicated, and extremely hard work, although some writers tried to find a romantic side to it, as witnessed by 'A Washing-Day Song' which appeared in *The Girl's Own Paper* of 1900.

> Soap and rub, sing and scrub,
> Sing at the washing-tub,
> Joyful in drudgery, queen of your toil;
> Sordid the slop and steam,
> White as a hawthorn dream
> Shall its fair outcome seem,
> Linen immaculate, guiltless of soil.
> Souse and swing, rinse and wring,

Over the mangle sing,
Let no reluctant frown gladness despoil;
What though the back rebel?
Tired fingers ache and swell?
Sing! you shall conquer well,
Queen of your toil!
Soap and rub, sing and scrub,
Sing at the washing-tub,
Joyful in drudgery, queen of your toil!

A wringer

Bradford's Patent Vowel Washing Machine

The Barnes' Patent Clothes Dryer and Airer

Notes and References

1 *The Lady's Dressing-Room,* op. cit.
2 Flora Thompson, *Lark Rise to Candleford,* 1939.
3 *The Girl's Own Paper,* 1880.
4 Ibid.
5 Ibid., 1889.
6 Ibid., 1899.
7 D. H. Lawrence, *The Rainbow,* 1915.
8 *The Girl's Own Paper,* 1894.
9 *Lark Rise to Candleford,* op. cit.
10 *The Girl's Own Paper,* 1892.
11 Ibid., 1880.
12 Ibid.
13 *Lark Rise to Candleford,* op. cit.
14 Charles Dickens, *Bleak House,* 1853.
15 *The Girl's Own Paper,* 1880.
16 *The Workwoman's Guide,* op. cit.
17 *The Girl's Own Paper,* 1880.
18 *Lark Rise to Candleford,* op. cit.
19 *The Girl's Own Paper,* 1892.
20 Ibid.
21 Ibid., 1880.
22 *Enquire Within,* 1893.
23 Ibid., 1894.
24 Ibid.
25 *Home Notes,* 1894.
26 *The Girl's Own Paper,* 1893.
27 Ibid., 1892.
28 Ibid.
29 Ibid., 1877.
30 *Home Notes,* 1894.
31 *Lark Rise to Candleford,* op. cit.
32 *Home Notes,* 1894.
33 *Lark Rise to Candleford,* op. cit.
34 *The Girl's Own Paper,* 1880.
35 Ibid.
36 Ibid.
37 Ibid.

4
Caps and Hats

'Males and females alike, we had always to wear something on our heads out of doors. Even for children playing in the garden, this was absolutely necessary. According to the weather, we were told, that we should catch cold, or get sunstroke, if we went bareheaded. But the real reason was that it was proper – that the hat was an essential part of the dress.'[1]

So wrote Gwen Raverat, recalling her youth in the 1890s, but she could have been speaking of any time in the Victorian period. Indeed, she should have been grateful that she was brought up in the latter part of the nineteenth century, when it was necessary to cover the head only when outside or in public. Until the 1860s, at least, it was usual for most women to wear some form of head covering both outdoors and indoors for virtually twenty-four hours a day.

CAPS

During the morning, the lady of the house generally attended to domestic affairs, visiting the children in the nursery, seeing to the garden, overseeing the cleaning of the house, or arranging the menus for the day. For such occupations she needed to be neat but not dressy, and she was advised to wear a simple gown and to tidy her hair away under a 'muslin or lace cap of no pretensions'.[2] Despite this advice, many such 'morning caps' were more decorative than functional, perching on top of the head rather than covering the hair, and displaying frills and insertions of lace and openwork embroidery, and rosettes and streamers of silk ribbon.

In overall design, morning caps followed closely the changing shapes of contemporary bonnets. In 1837, they were made of white lawn or muslin, and enveloped most of the head, with layers of stiffened frills forming a halo round the face. By the 1840s they had become more close-fitting, their frills and silk ribbons hanging down over the ears in the form of lappets, while during the following decade they grew smaller and less bonnet-like, and were worn further back on the head. At this time, too, a greater range of materials was used, and caps made of crocheted cotton, lace, or lace and embroidery, showed a new lightness and delicacy. By 1860, a popular form was the 'fanchon', which was nothing more than a triangle of muslin which perched on top of the head, with the point at the front and long streamers at the back.

During the late 1860s and early 1870s, a variety of shapes and styles was worn, ranging from small pieces of fabric, like the fanchon, to a soft, full-crowned muslin cap of the 'seventies called the 'Charlotte Corday'. Many of this decade followed bonnet styles in adopting long lace or muslin strings, which tied loosely under the chin. After the middle of the century, however, younger women began to stop wearing caps, and, by about 1880, they were almost entirely reserved for the elderly.

While caps were in fashion, it was essential that they be clean and crisp. 'They must be very fresh, elegant, and choice, or they are positively disfiguring.'[3] They were *never* to be used as an excuse for hiding untidy hair, as was the wont of one Bertha, cited in *The Ladies' Treasury* of 1857. 'She had nice hair, but now she neglects it, pops on a very unbecoming cap, not over nice, and rushes down to breakfast, to disenchant her husband, and make him wonder how he could have been weak enough to marry her.'[4]

Afternoons required more formal dress, for this was the time for giving and receiving calls. Visiting between neighbours and relatives was considered a matter of common courtesy, and a duty necessary 'to maintain good feeling between the members of society'.[5] In an age before the telephone was in general use, a personal call was the only method of exchanging intimate news and gossip, and was the accepted means of delivering invitations

Lady's morning cap of white muslin and silk ribbon (1849)

for formal social engagements, and for thanking the host after the event. Thus, around midday, the well-to-do lady of the house would change her complete outfit, donning a silk dress and a more elaborate 'dress' cap, in which she could appear to visitors. (Female visitors might either keep their bonnets on for the length of the call, or bring their caps with them, in special baskets.) Her poorer cousins, however, who could not afford so many gowns, relied solely on the change of cap, in the same way as the ladies of Cranford, as described by Mrs Gaskell. 'The expenditure on dress in Cranford was principally in that one article referred to. If the heads were buried in smart new caps, the ladies were like ostriches and cared not what became of their bodies.' [6] Thus, in the morning, Miss Matty wore 'a cap with yellow ribbons that had been Miss Jenkyns' best, and which Miss Matty was wearing out in private,' but for the afternoon, 'when she expected to be seen,' she wore a grander version, 'made in imitation of Mrs. Jamieson's'.[7]

Still more elaborate dress caps were worn in the evening for dinner parties, concerts, balls and the like. These might range in form from the full turban, still popular in 1837, to a mere scattering of jewels, flowers and feathers, but, in general, formal caps followed the same lines as the informal caps.

Until the 1850s, the afternoon caps were bonnets of lace, net or gauze, trimmed with gauze ribbon or silk 'blonde' lace, while tiny fanchons with lappets were worn for evening. By the late 1850s, all caps were smaller, and worn further back on the head, and the popular evening style was the 'cachepeigne', a stiffened crescent of net, trimmed with ribbons. Around 1860, the hair was worn in a heavy chignon which hung down to the shoulders, and this was often enclosed in a chenille net snood. A coronet of velvet, trimmed with lace, flowers or beads, was now worn for evening.

During the next few years, trimmings became stiffer and heavier, with much use of satin and velvet ribbons. A typical dinner cap of the late 1860s, as described in *The Englishwoman's Domestic Magazine* of 1868, consisted of scarlet velvet ribbons, covered with lace insertions, and edged at the back with guipure lace. The sides were trimmed with lace rosettes, and from these hung white satin ribbons tied under the chignon.

In the 1870s, dress caps were usually of stiffened velvet or lace with raised crowns, and were often beaded, so that they were virtually indistinguishable from contemporary bonnets and hats. From the 1880s, however, dress caps, like morning caps, disappeared almost completely from fashionable circles.

At the end of the evening, when the Victorian woman took off her dress cap and retired to bed, she donned a third head covering, the nightcap. These were usually of white lawn or muslin, covering most of the head, fitting at the back by means of a drawstring and tying under the chin at the front. Not surprisingly they were the least subject to the influences of fashion, remaining predominantly plain and functional, their only decoration a row of frills or some insertions of lace or openwork embroidery. Their chief requirement was that they should stay on, and *The Workwoman's Guide* (1838) had a pattern for 'a very neat nightcap', which 'when made of checked muslin, with a border of corded muslin, has a very pretty appearance, and is particularly comfortable for a night-cap, as it sits close to the head.' These, too, went out of fashion after 1880.

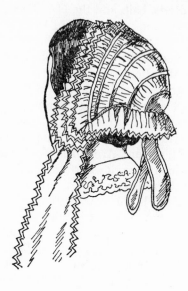

Lady's cambric nightcap (1857)

BONNETS AND HATS

Out of doors, some sort of headgear was essential at all times, and the most popular form for the Victorian woman was the bonnet. Both bonnets and hats had been fashionable during the first quarter of the century, but from the 1830s to the 1860s, hats went out of fashion completely, and were worn only with the masculine-style riding habit, or for extremely informal pursuits such as gardening or walks by the seaside. They were adopted again in the 'fifties by younger women, but were still considered sporty and rather 'fast'. It was not until the late 1860s that hats were once again as fashionable as bonnets, and by the last two decades of the century changes in style had made them virtually indistinguishable.

The most popular material for both bonnets and hats was stiffened, plaited straw. This was worn during the summer months, with walking dress, by the very fashionable, and at all times by the less well-to-do. In fact, England had a thriving straw hat industry, based on the counties of Bedfordshire, Hertfordshire and Buckinghamshire, where locally grown wheat was plaited by women and children, working in their own homes. The straws, plaits, and finished bonnets and hats were sold through the markets of St Albans, Dunstable and Luton.

In terms of fineness, colour and durability, however, English straw bonnets could not compare with those imported from Italy, particularly those from Tuscany called 'leghorns'. Although expensive, they were much sought after by the fashion-conscious lady of the mid-nineteenth century, and Mrs Gaskell, writing in 1852, proclaimed that 'my sole want in the world in the dress line is a leghorn bonnet, and that I fear is not likely to be cheaper at London or Paris than here.'[8]

Also popular were a whole range of variations on the straw bonnet, using materials such as paper, grass, rushes, whalebone, horsehair, and chip. The latter, made from the shavings of young white-wood trees, such as lime, poplar or willow, was a particular favourite. After the middle of the century, felt was much used for women's hats, and other materials like silk, velvet and tulle could also be used if they were mounted on a stiffened foundation. One popular version was the 'drawn silk' bonnet, where the fabric was gathered over cane or wire hoops, producing a surface of puffs and ruches.

The most important feature of the Victorian bonnet or hat was its trimmings, for it was these which made it so feminine, and so versatile. According to one writer, fashion demanded that every woman 'have a hat or bonnet to match each dress in the wardrobe'.[9] Naturally, for most women, this was financially impossible, but by the addition of a few ribbons, flowers or feathers of the right colour, a basic straw bonnet or felt hat could be made to match any outfit. These trimmings could be bought quite cheaply, and could be transferred from the winter bonnet to the summer one at the end of the season. 'You may take the trimming off the felt, brush the hat, and put it carefully away till autumn, and transfer the silk trimming and a feather to a coarse brown straw hat, which will cost 2s. or 3s. With a bow of amber silk, it will look very pretty, and will harmonise with your cashmere, or your stone-coloured beige.'[10]

The other important feature of the bonnet was the lining of the brim, for until the 1860s, when bonnets finally receded to the back of the head, bonnet brims provided a frame for the face, and their decoration was thus very important. 'Linings, therefore, as well as transparent bonnets, have a great effect on the complexion; they must not be considered only as the frame that is best suited to the picture, but rather as the drapery that is to give proper light and shade so to supply the tint that is deficient in the face, and steal away any harsh or over-prominent hues.'[11] Silk linings, flowers, ribbons and beads were all used to decorate the inside of the brim, and in many cases as much trouble was spent on the inside as on the outside.

This was especially so at the beginning of Victoria's reign. At this time the bonnet was large, with a deep crown tilting upwards from the back of the head like an upturned flower pot, and the brim wide and slanted at a similar angle at the front. It was tied with wide ribbons under the chin, which pulled in the sides of the bonnet and allowed the brim to form a large oval frame to the face. A curtain of fabric, called a bavolet, was attached to the base of the crown to cover and protect the back of the neck. Straw and velvet were both used for bonnets, but light nets, tulle, and, in particular, silk, were also very popular. Trimmings of silk ribbons, flowers and feathers were used to adorn the crown and the inside of the brim.

After 1838 a new bonnet shape appeared, which was more in keeping with the subdued look of the 1840s. The brim and crown united to form a continuous horizontal tube, but with the brim curving down in wings at the side of the face and reaching to well below the level of the chin. The effect was to hide the profile of the wearer so that her face was visible only from the front, where her neatly parted hair and side ringlets were framed by the lining and the trimmings on the inside of the bonnet. Peeping out from such a setting, the wearer appeared both modest and coy, causing one writer to note that 'The form of straw bonnets are at the present moment extremely coquettish.'[12]

From the mid 'forties onwards, openwork straw and fancy braids, or a mixture of straw and horsehair, produced bonnets that were exquisitely delicate and lacey. Chip bonnets were also very fashionable at this time. Trimmings were usually centred on the sides of the bonnet, and consisted of rosettes of ribbon or a curling ostrich plume, while in the summer flowers and grasses were suitably seasonal – 'Bonnet of fancy straw, decorated with pink plaid ribbon, and a cluster of small pink shaded roses, encircled with wheatears, small roses decorating the interior.'[13]

With the softer, more expansive styles of the 1850s, the form of the bonnet changed. The crown diminished and the brim shortened so that the whole thing slid to the back of the head, revealing the face and hair. From the front, all that could be seen of the bonnet was the ribbon bow under the chin and the trimmings inside the brim, which thus formed a decorative halo round the head. In this diminutive form the bonnet itself was little more than a foundation for layers of silk and velvet ribbon, black lace, blonde, feathers and flowers.

As skirts grew wider in the late 1850s, bringing a greater emphasis on the horizontal line, bonnets flattened on the top of the head and the trimmings were concentrated at the sides and on the long bavolet at the back.

This horizontal emphasis was also echoed in the return of the hat, in a form which was wide and low-crowned. Hats had been worn during the 1840s in the country or at the seaside, but they had been chiefly functional, shading the face and neck from the sun and safeguarding the fashionably pale complexion. To achieve this, they were circular and rather flat, with a low crown, the shape reminiscent of an inverted saucer. The late 1850s saw this flat hat enter the semi-formal realms of promenade and carriage costume, where, made of silk, with hanging ribbons and sporting an ostrich plume, it was given the dashing name of 'mousquetaire' hat. Then, in the 1860s, smaller versions became general fashionable wear, for a small neat head provided a balance to the huge crinoline skirt, which reached its maximum width at this time. The whole effect was completely different from the bonnets of the previous decades, for without bonnet strings, curving sides and bavolet to frame the face and enclose the hair, there was a new freedom about the head.

The hats were themselves jaunty in style, and sometimes rather masculine. Small, low-crowned hats had narrow brims, turned up at the sides and pointing down at front and back. 'Coolie' hats, like little plates, were thought to be in the Japanese style, and 'Scotch caps' were based on the Highlander's bonnet. A variety of materials was used. Straw and chip were still predominant, but other

Bonnet of straw and silk with flower trimmings (1864)

fabrics were also being explored, particularly for winter. Thus, in November 1861, *The Englishwoman's Domestic Magazine* noted: 'The fashionable hats are the Tudor, the Garibaldi, and Diadem, which during the summer have been made in straw and crinoline, but have now appeared in felt and velvet.'

The use of felt was a completely new departure. Prior to this, felt had been reserved almost entirely for riding hats, where its smooth angular forms matched the neat, crisp lines of the riding habits. Now, its masculine qualities were ideally suited to the new jaunty style, and it appeared in numerous little hats with high crowns and turned up brims. Velvet was also particularly popular, and was used to line or trim a whole range of different hats. Per-

Lady's hat of white chip
bound with silk, trimmed with lace,
feathers, roses and ribbons (1857)

haps most typical of the 1860s, however, was its use in the 'pork-pie', a small pill-box shaped hat with a turned up brim lying almost flush with the sides of the crown. This was usually made of black velvet, trimmed with one or two small feathers in red or white, and was often worn perched on top of the snood.

Despite the growing popularity of the hat amongst the young, bonnets were still in the majority. In the early 1860s they grew narrower, and rose at the front in a spoon-shaped brim, which was filled with trimmings. During the next few years, hairstyles changed, and the chignon, which had been low on the neck, rose to the crown of the head. The bonnet was lifted at the back until, from 1867, it lay flat on the head, the strings tying either under the chin or behind the chignon. At the same time bonnets grew smaller, until by 1866 they were 'mere ornamental coiffures, showing to great advantage the hair and the face when it is young and beautiful; and ladies have a dread of ensconcing their pretty features once more in large poky bonnets.'[14] Made of velvet, straw, silk, or even felt, they were trimmed with lace, flowers, velvet ribbons, feathers and beads.

The general look of the early 1870s was curvaceous and frothy, and hairstyles grew still more voluminous. Aided by artificial 'scalpettes' and 'frizettes', the hair now hung down to the shoulders in coils and ringlets. Hats were worn tilted forward on the front of the head at a coquettish angle, and often trailed ribbons at the back. Bonnets, on the other hand, grew sufficiently large, after 1873, to move to the back of the head and enclose the upper half of the chignon. The most popular bonnet shape had a round crown and an upturned brim in the form of a diadem. Both hats and bonnets were smothered in trimmings, which were even more profuse than those of previous decades. Artificial flowers became particularly popular, so that in 1875 *The Englishwoman's Domestic Magazine* said that 'Flowers, and nothing but flowers are all the ornament of our chapeaux,' although, in fact, lace, ribbon bows and feathers were still worn too. Under this mass of ornament it was difficult to differentiate between hats and bonnets, and when, in the middle of the decade, many bonnets were worn without strings, they were virtually indistinguishable. By the 1880s, however, bonnets were again worn with wide ribbon ties under the chin.

During the 1880s, the female silhouette was long and narrow, with a bustle that was sharply angular, and hats and bonnets reflected this mood. Typical was the 'postilion' or 'post-boy' hat, its tall crown shaped like an upturned flower-pot, and with a narrow brim, often turned up at the sides or back. It was worn flat on top of the head, with all the back hair now swept up inside the crown and just a curly fringe showing at the front. This upward movement was also displayed in tall-crowned, wide-brimmed 'Gainsborough' hats, their brims turned up at one side in cavalier fashion. The tendency was towards angular, more masculine hats and, of course, it was in the late 1880s that sailor hats, known today as straw boaters, were first 'worn by the million' for walking, cycling and other outdoor pursuits. More feminine styles were retained, however, in the form of small toques and bonnets, although these reflected the same upward movement with higher crowns, and often had brims forming a pointed arch at the front.

Straw was more popular than ever, and was now worn all the year round, with openwork plaits and fancy braids revived for bonnets. Velvet and plush, the typical fabrics of the 1880s, were both used, the former often in conjunction with straw. *The Woman's World* of 1888 noted that 'vast numbers of straw bonnets are made with rows of velvet alternating with the straw.'

Trimmings still included ribbons and artificial flowers, and, on bonnets, beads provided additional glitter and contrast, but the most characteristic feature of the late 1870s and 1880s was the use of feathers. Odd plumes had long been popular, but in this period aigrettes, wings and even whole birds were used. Some toques were made entirely from feathers, while *The Ladies' Treasury* of 1882 described a 'Bonnet of coarse fancy straw on which a white cockatoo nestles.' When hats and bonnets grew smaller in the late 1880s, the illusion of height was retained by the use of tall, pointed feather trimmings. Single plumes, or pairs of wings, rose vertically from the front of the crown, or whole birds arched their wings upwards as if about to launch themselves from the top of the wearer's head.

By the 1890s, bonnets had virtually disappeared, except amongst older women, but a wide variety of hats was worn. They ranged from small confections of wired velvet with beads and up-standing feathers 'like question marks,'[15] to almost plain, boat-shaped, felt hats for walking and cycling. Straw sailor hats were now worn for general wear, and from 1896 a felt hat, very like a man's trilby, became fashionable. Yet wide-brimmed hats were still worn too, and were growing wider. Gwen Raverat remembered these 'enormous over-trimmed hats, which were fixed to the armature of one's puffed-out hair by long and murderous pins. On the top of an open bus, in a wind, their mighty sails flapped agonizingly at their anchorage, and pulled out one's hair by the handful.'[16] These were to be the dominant style of the early 1900s.

CARE AND CLEANING

Despite their elaboration, the Victorian housewife was as ready to clean her caps and hats as any other item of her wardrobe.

The plainer morning caps and nightcaps could be put in the family wash, and then starched and ironed along with the other linens, but dress caps were more difficult to deal with, since they combined such a variety of materials. In many cases the only way was to unpick the lace, ribbons, feathers, artificial flowers, etc., and either replace them with new ones or clean them all separately. The same applied to hat trimmings.

Once the trimmings had been removed, the basic foundation materials of bonnets and hats could usually be cleaned. Some types were more easily soiled than others. Straw, although so popular, had the disadvantage that apart from being subject to general soiling, and to dirt particles lodging in the straw plaits, it was easily discoloured by the action of the sun and tended to go limp in the rain. If a straw bonnet were really discoloured, *The Workwoman's Guide* recommended that it be 'picked to pieces, and the plat turned, so that which was inside is then outwards', but even so, 'the bonnet should be cleaned well before being unpicked.'

White straw bonnets and hats – never really white, but bleached lighter than the natural straw colour – were the most difficult to keep clean. *Home Notes* recommended a mixture of one pennyworth of oxalic acid in half a pint of boiling water: 'with a piece of flannel, rub the hat well all over, using the acid as hot as the hand can bear. After thoroughly rubbing, rinse the hat in cold water and dry, taking care to keep the shape. When dry the straw will be found to be as clean and crisp as new.'[17] Another method, recommended for leghorn hats, was to wash them with a solution of hot potash water. If the chief problem was straightforward dust, then scrubbing with a nail brush and salt water was all that was needed, but if the hats were really discoloured the usual method was to bleach them with sulphur. The simple method was to 'rub the straw with cut lemon dipped in sulphur, and wash the juice off carefully with water.' [18] The more complicated version, closer to that used to bleach the original unplaited straw, involved placing the hat in the vicinity of burning sulphur. The hat was first washed in soapy water, and allowed to half dry. 'Then put a little sulphur in paper. Stand the hat on a two-pound preserve jar, put the sulphur by the side, have ready a large washing mug to put over the hat, light the paper, and put the mug down before the light catches the sulphur, and let it stand all night under the mug. You will find this will make the hat like new.' [19]

With black straw that had become dirty or dingy there were two alternatives. Either the hat could be cleaned with diluted oxalic acid, in which case the colour was bleached to 'a very good brown'; [20] or, if the owner wished to keep her hat black, she could paint it with a home-made blacking mixture. One recipe required that the straw be brushed all over the outside with equal parts of black ink and sweet oil, then rubbed with a cloth. More often recommended was a solution of half an ounce of best black sealing wax in two ounces of turpentine or spirits of wine. A bottle containing these two ingredients was placed near the fire, or in boiling water, until the wax melted, care being taken that the spirit itself did not ignite. The wax solution was then spread on the hat with a toothbrush, the hat being held near the fire all the time in order to keep the wax soft. When dry, this varnish gave 'a beautiful gloss and stiffness' [21] and also made the hat waterproof.

As for coloured straws, these could be 'freshened, if not too discoloured, faded, or burnt, by dipping a cloth into hot water containing one tablespoonful of liquid ammonia to the pint. When the cloth is wrung out it is placed on the brim of the hat, which is laid flat side down on to a table, and the brim pressed with a warm but not too hot iron. The iron must not be left too long on the hat, or the colour will be affected.' [22]

Straw hats and bonnets become limp very easily, especially in wet weather. According to *Enquire Within* of 1894, 'A straw hat that has lost its shape, or has the brim or crown bent or sunken by an impromptu shower, may be restored by setting the hat over a steaming kettle, and shaping it when moist as it is desired to have it, then setting it in the air to dry quickly.' Flat brims and simple hat shapes which had been warped by rain, or by the process of cleaning, could be remodelled by being re-dampened, covered with a fine cloth or handkerchief, and pressed with a box iron. The crown of a hat or bonnet could be reshaped by drying it on a block, but an alternative to this was to pin it down over another hat of the same shape. The flower-pot-shaped crowns of the 1880s could be fitted over the end of a jug, jar or bottle, to maintain the shape during cleaning, and then the hat left to dry upside down with the jar still inside it. 'This process should be slowly affected, and away from the fire, so that it should not become warped.' [23]

Sometimes the process of wetting and cleaning removed the original stiffening, and the straw had to be re-treated before shaping. Various stiffening agents were available. *Home Notes* of 1895 recommended brushing the straw with 'the white of an egg beaten to a froth'. Starch was sometimes used, while *The Workwoman's Guide* favoured glue: 'The best stiffening is that made of buffalo's hide or vellum which may be procured in London and Liverpool, cut into shreds, and sold at 8d. a pound.' A quarter of a pound of these, when boiled in two quarts of water for six or seven hours, produced a jelly which was a highly efficient, if somewhat smelly, form of stiffening agent. Ivory shavings or bone dust could be used in the same way, while 'isinglass for best, and white glue for common bonnets' [24] were also recommended. After being brushed with one of these solutions, the bonnet was held near the fire for a few minutes, pulled into shape, and then hung up to dry for about six hours.

Felt hats were generally much easier to clean than straw, and both wet and dry cleaning methods could be used. On the one hand, they could be sponged with a strong solution of ammonia, or soda dissolved in water. Alternatively, a dry cleaning agent such as Benzine collas could be used, but to protect the wearer from lingering fumes it was advisable to wipe the hat with a clean damp sponge afterwards, and dry it in the open air. The other basic method was to cover the hat with a powder which absorbed the grease and dirt and could then be brushed off. The type of powder varied according to the colour of the felt. For white felt, powdered pipe-clay, or a paste of magnesia and water, spread on and allowed to dry, were both equally recommended. For light brown or fawn, fuller's earth or oatmeal were used, 'made hot and applied with a flannel'.[25] By the same principle, 'Slightly soiled grey felts may be cleaned with warm bran,'[26] although if really dirty, a wet cleaning solution of pearl-ash and water was the only remedy. This latter mixture could also be used for red felt, 'but if the colour is not fast it is best to try the solution on the interior of the hat, or a part that may afterwards be trimmed over, if the colour should fade.'[27]

Black felts, however, were treated quite differently, being first brushed to remove the dust, then covered with a liquid that was really a dye rather than a cleaning solution. It consisted of 'a pennyworth of logwood and a pennyworth of soap bark'[28] cut into chips and steeped in boiling water. After leaving them to stand for five minutes, the liquid was drained off and applied to the hat while still hot.

Other materials used in the making and trimming of hats, such as velvet, silk and crape, were cleaned by the same methods as dresses made of these fabrics. Lace frills, and feather plumes and tips, would be taken off and given the usual treatment for lace and feathers, before being replaced or transferred to a new hat. Silk ribbons were cleaned with honey, soap and gin, just like silk dresses, but white satin ribbons could also be washed with a strong lather of best white soap and clear cold water. The important thing to remember with satin ribbons was not to rub them, as they frayed very easily. The method of pressing was also crucial. One recipe advised steaming as being 'much better for the purpose than the pressure of an iron',[29] but an alternative method was to let the ribbon half dry on a line, and then to put it between clean cloths and iron it by drawing the ribbon from under the iron, 'this prevents creasing and a stringy appearance at finish.'[30] With white satin, rinsing was sometimes avoided so that 'the suds that remain in the ribbon will give it the proper degree of stiffness,'[31] and it was then ironed while still wet. However, we are told that 'None but satin ribbon of the thickest and best quality can be washed to any advantage.'[32]

Finally, although artificial flowers could not really be cleaned, 'Good flowers, if not very faded and very dirty, may have some of their pristine freshness restored by steaming and cutting the crumpled edges.'[33]

Notes and References

1 Gwen Raverat, *Period Piece*, 1952.
2 Anon., *Elegant Arts for Ladies, c.* 1856.
3 *The Ladies' Treasury*, 1857.
4 Ibid.
5 *Elegant Arts for Ladies*, op. cit.
6 Elizabeth Gaskell, *Cranford*, 1853.
7 Ibid.
8 J. A. V. Chapple and Arthur Pollard (eds.), *The Letters of Mrs. Gaskell*, 1966.
9 *How to Dress Well on A Shilling A Day*, op. cit.
10 Ibid.
11 Mrs M. J. Howell, *The Handbook of Millinery*, 1847.
12 *The World of Fashion*, 1846.
13 Ibid.
14 *The Englishwoman's Domestic Magazine*, 1866.
15 *The Queen*, 1896.
16 *Period Piece*, op. cit.
17 *Home Notes*, 1894.
18 Ibid., 1895.
19 *Enquire Within*, 1892.
20 *Home Notes*, 1894.
21 Clare Hill, *Millinery Theoretical and Practical*, 1900.
22 *The Workwoman's Guide*, op. cit.
23 *The Girl's Own Paper*, 1887.
24 *The Workwoman's Guide*, op. cit.
25 *Millinery Theoretical and Practical*, op. cit.
26 Ibid.
27 Ibid.
28 Ibid.
29 *Enquire Within*, 1894.
30 *Millinery Theoretical and Practical*, op. cit.
31 *Miss Leslie's Magazine*, 1843.
32 Ibid.
33 *Millinery Theoretical and Practical*, op. cit.

5
Gloves and Footwear

GLOVES

The Victorian lady, anxious to preserve the colour and texture of her hands in a cold and grimy world, spent the greater proportion of her waking life in gloves. Far from being confined to outdoor wear, these were considered 'graceful at all times for a lady in the house,'[1] the only universal exception being that 'when a lady has taken her seat at the dinner table she should at once remove her gloves.'[2] Her hands remained covered on all other social occasions, whether informal visits or evening balls, and only as a mark of the utmost friendship did she remove a glove to shake hands. Thus a girl of the 1850s who, suffering from the intense heat, had removed her gloves in church, was told severely that only the imminent danger of fainting could excuse such vulgar behaviour.[3]

Different styles and materials prevailed according to when and where the gloves were to be worn. 'If they are required for town, of course they must be kid in summer, and for the winter double-sewn calf or dog-skin answer well. . . . For a country life, untanned garden gauntlets are the most suitable.'[4] Large numbers were needed – according to one estimate the absolute minimum was 'six pairs of kid gloves and one pair of double-sewn dog-skin; but I think that for those living in the country this should be amended to only four pairs of kid (including those for evening wear), two double-sewn and two pairs of gauntlets.'[5] In *Period Piece*, Gwen Raverat recalls her bitter resentment at having to spend her precious allowance on 'lots of long white kid gloves, which were very expensive; and never nice again after they had once got dirty'; her feelings must have been shared by innumerable women struggling to be smart on a small budget.

At the beginning of the period, day gloves were of buff or yellow kid, wrist-length, and fastened with one button. A suitable colour could be obtained at home by dyeing an old pair of white gloves with an infusion of saffron – 'the tops should be previously sewed up, to prevent the colour getting in.'[6] In the 'fifties, 'gloves should be in the most delicate tints that can be procured,'[7] but a decade later they had become more fancy, with bright blue or green in favour, and the wrist edge either scalloped or narrowly banded with white. This last had its disadvantages, however, as it quickly became dirty and looked shabby. From the middle of the 1860s day gloves lengthened; by 1873 'the glove should be fully long enough to come over the wrist, and should have two or three buttons; otherwise the hand will look short and thick;'[8] it might even extend to eight- or ten-button length. Gloves of the 'eighties were longer still, even covering the elbow when worn with short-sleeved dresses, but in the following decade the four-button length was usual again.

Evening dresses were always more or less short-sleeved, and the gloves worn with them were correspondingly longer. For the first ten years of the period they covered approximately one-third of the lower arm, and were fastened with two to four buttons. They were usually made of white kid, though pale pink or yellow were also permitted; they were sometimes embroidered on the back of the hand, or trimmed round the top with lace or ribbon. By the mid 1860s they had lengthened to four, five or six buttons, and by the 'seventies 'gloves are worn larger than ever, and generally of dull kid, with as many as eight or ten buttons for ball toilettes, the bracelet being put on *over* the glove.'[9] Unless the dress was pure white, 'gloves of the very palest shade of primrose, which look white by gaslight, are more becoming than the dead white kid, and last longer.'[10] Evening gloves reached their maximum length in the 1880s, fastening with up to twenty buttons, although they often had an opening at the wrist only, closed with four. 'Ladies whose arms are not well-turned and white should always wear long gloves at balls and dinners. If desired, these gloves can meet the short sleeves of the dress, or they may extend only to the elbow.'[11] Lace

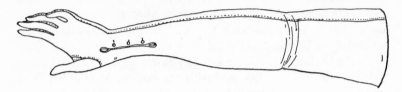

Lady's suede glove (1895)

or embroidered trimming were common, and grey, cream, tan or black were as much worn as white. Kid was the usual material, the Swedish variety being admired for its scent, although 'French kid wears better than Swedish, Danish, or Brussels.'[12] Suede enjoyed great popularity from the 1860s, until Queen Victoria banned it from her drawing-rooms in 1882. Silk was fashionable for most of the 'eighties, and won the approval of doctors: 'I think it always wholesomer to wear silk than kid gloves, especially in the evening, and at balls, when the skin is particularly apt to become hot, and to transpire freely. Long silk gloves are now largely worn, both indoors and out, and I rejoice at the fashion, for it is eminently sensible and hygienic.'[13]

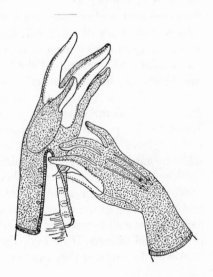

Lady's doeskin gloves
with leather palms,
for riding and driving (1895)

For country wear, silk, cotton and the stouter leathers were worn throughout the period, while gauntlet gloves lined with fur or wool were popular for travelling and riding. Netted mittens were fashionable until the end of the 1840s. Of black or white silk with the backs lightly embroidered, they reached to the wrist for day wear and halfway to the elbow for evening. During the 1850s and 1860s they continued to be worn, but were no longer strictly fashionable; they returned for evening wear in the late 'seventies and 'eighties, now in machine-knitted openwork and longer in length, and of a colour to match the dress, and won approval because '[their] use . . . obviates the necessity of baring the arms at dinner or supper.'[14]

FOOTWEAR

From the beginning of the period until about 1860, shoes were slim and heelless. For day wear they were of neutral-coloured cloth or leather, while for evening black or white satin prevailed. In the late 1840s there was a brief revival of coloured evening shoes in figured satin or embroidered canvas, but by the following decade neutral shades were once more in favour: 'Coloured shoes, we need scarcely say, are exceedingly vulgar; delicate pink, and faint blue silk, for these articles, have numerous advocates: but white satin, black satin, or kid, and bronze kid, are neater and more elegant than any other colour or material.'[15] Boots for evening wear were made up in the same materials and colours. Stockings were similarly unobtrusive: 'On ordinary occasions white stockings harmonize best with the colour of the dress, unless it be of black, when, of course, black stockings will be worn.'[16] They were made of silk, or a mixture of silk and cotton, and the decoration ranged from a simple clock to more elaborate openwork and embroidery.

Heels began to appear on shoes from the 1850s, at first only for day wear. They averaged one inch, but even this modest height was viewed with some alarm. 'I am sure you had too high-heeled boots,' wrote Queen Victoria anxiously to her daughter, who had sprained her foot.[17] By the 'sixties heels were general. The advent of the wire crinoline in the second half of the 'fifties, which by its uncontrollable movements brought both feet and ankles clearly, if fitfully, into view, resulted in the exuberant footwear of the 1860s: 'A great revolution has taken place in the chaussure of ladies, which, generally speaking, admits of but little variety. For the black shoe or boot, which used to be worn on nearly all occasions, coloured ones are substituted, to accord nicely with the dress with which they are worn. For house shoes we have noticed some, made with high heels, in blue, violet, scarlet, and green morocco. These are generally worn with silk or cotton stockings spotted with the colour of the morocco.'[18] White silk stockings were, however, still worn for formal occasions, and indoor shoes of bronze kid retained their popularity until the end of the period.

From the 1870s until the end of the period, heels adopted the characteristic 'Louis' shape, slim and waisted, and rose to one-and-a-half or two inches, to the outrage of the medical profession: 'The absurd and ungainly practice of mounting the hinder part of the feet on stilts whilst the toes press the ground and bear the weight, is one against which it is not easy to write with temper. The device of strangling the waist with tightly-laced corsets was contemptible for its ignorance; that to which we now allude is outrageous in its defiance of the laws of gravity. . . . A moment's reflection should lead to the instant abandonment of a practice so manifestly irrational and ridiculous; but, forsooth, the foot looks somewhat smaller as seen from the front or side when placed obliquely; so, regardless of common sense and common prudence, the practice prevails. Such is the folly and wantonness of vanity!'[19] At the same time the toes became increasingly pointed, and lengthened throughout the next two decades. Great attention was paid to trimming; thus the hard-up were told reassuringly that 'nice shoes need not cost more than 2/6, and these, with a bow, made up of any old scrap of ribbon, and set off with good steel buckles, will always look nice. A pair of buckles, if care be taken to keep them bright, will last for ever, and improve the appearance of both shoe and foot immensely: they cost between four and five shillings.'[20] Stockings were coloured to match the dress for day wear, and stripes were popular, although they tended to 'wear unequally, and give where the stripes meet'.[21] Evening stockings were white, or at least very pale; 'the most elegant are of course of silk, and have very often clocks of Valenciennes lace and initials embroidered in silk.'[22]

Shoes of the 1880s were often decorated with multiple bars, and at the beginning of the 'nineties bead embroidery and cut-outs over a contrasting colour were popular. But the 1890s also saw a return to simplicity in footwear; many shoes were plain, with only a small buckle for trimming, and although some stockings were enriched with lace and even hand-painted, 'there are many ladies of good taste who prefer to wear black open-worked stockings and black shoes with all dresses in the evening, and black patent slippers for the daytime, with black hose.' [23]

Outdoor footwear was quite different from indoor. Already by the beginning of the period, 'the insane practice that formerly prevailed of ladies walking the streets in winter with their feet *chaussé* as for a ballroom, in open-clocked silk stockings, and light kid shoes, has most fortunately subsided; and has long since been wisely replaced by cotton or merino stockings, india-rubbers, double-soles, and gaiter-boots.' [24] A typical early Victorian walking boot was of neutral-coloured cloth with a black leather toe-cap, ankle-length and laced up the inside. An elastic-sided boot was patented in 1837 and was worn for at least the next thirty years, being much patronized by Her Majesty. By the early 'sixties heels were found on boots as well as shoes, and the boots of the 'sixties followed the general trend of that decade, with very bright colours and tassel trimmings. From the late 'sixties they laced up the front or buttoned up the side with numerous small buttons requiring a special hook. In the second half of the period, boots ceased to be

A combined shoehorn and button-hook

worn indoors and were made exclusively for outdoor wear; they were of cloth or leather, usually black, and they grew taller in the 'eighties and 'nineties, reaching halfway up the lower leg.

Stockings were held up by garters worn above the knee, 'and it is only in out-of-the-way country parts that to do this cords, tapes, and bits of string are sometimes used. The most humble servant-maid who is a little civilised buys elastic garters with buckles.

Everyone cannot bear a garter as tight as it should be. . . . In this case the stockings should be fastened to the stays by ribbons. But accidents might happen; for if the ribbon, which must be well stretched to hold up the stocking, were to break, down comes the stocking over the heel! My advice is to wear at the same time a garter not at all tight, but sufficiently so to hold up the stocking, in case of accidents, until the damage can be repaired. To wear the garter below the knee is against all rules of taste.' [25]

CARE AND CLEANING

Great importance was attached to the state of a lady's gloves, and 'a soiled glove, or one with a hole or a palpable repair, is quite inadmissible where you are paying a call or frequenting a public place.' [26] Care, time and money all had to be expended if the correct standard was to be maintained, for 'there is no more complete finish to dress than a good glove. . . . Gloves in former ages were embroidered with pearls and gems, and were costly property. Now-a-days, the excellence of their fit and their perfect freshness are their beauty.' [27] It is not surprising, therefore, that hints on glove-care were eagerly circulated.

Wear could be kept down if the gloves were well looked after to begin with. 'Remember to mend your gloves, and sew on the buttons when needed. Black kid should be rubbed with oil or butter, and a piece of flannel, before being worn; and when gloves require mending, they should be turned inside out, and sewn over and over on the wrong side. Small holes in them may be mended with court-plaister, so as to be invisible, and a little good black ink and oil will cover white marks caused by wear.' [28] White kid gloves required special treatment. It was impossible to prevent them from soiling; indeed the very rich threw them away as soon as they had lost their first freshness. But such extravagance was beyond the reach of most women. The glove had first to be held in shape, and for this purpose it was either put on the hand or onto a wooden glove-tree. It could then safely be cleaned by a variety of methods. It might be rubbed with cream of tartar, with stale bread, or with benzine. If it was very dirty, it could even be immersed in the benzine and dried in the open air to get rid of the smell. Spirits of hartshorn was an even better agent, as it left no smell at all. More simply, the gloves could be rubbed with 'a piece of moist flannel, on which a little powdered soap has been applied. When the dirt has been cleaned off the glove, the moisture is to be removed with a piece of dry flannel.' [29] If careless washing resulted in mildew stains, 'dry the gloves perfectly, stretch, rub the spots well with a rather stiff brush, and then with a small quantity of egg albumen or flour paste. This will not injure them, nor leave any unpleasant smell.' [30]

Different leathers could take different treatment. Suede could be cleaned with flour or dry bread, while 'the chamois gloves that are so fashionable may be made to look like new in the following way: Wash them in tepid, soft water, using plenty of Castile soap. Pull them out straight, and pass through a wringer. Rinse in water of the same temperature, straighten them, and pass through the wringer again. Shake them out well, and hang to dry in a cool shady place. Do not use hard water; rain water is better.' [31] The soap could be replaced by ammonia. Doeskin riding gloves were to be rubbed with dry fuller's earth and alum, and then sprinkled with dry bran and whiting; or they could be washed in tepid water and soap or bran tea, stretched on a hand and rubbed with a paste made up of colouring matter and beer or vinegar. 'If white, pipeclay should be used; light yellow gloves require yellow ochre to be mixed with the pipeclay; but if bright yellow, yellow ochre alone should be employed. When the gloves are dark-coloured, use a mixture of fuller's earth and rotten-stone.' [32] After this procedure had been gone through, the gloves had to be half-dried, smoothed and rubbed into shape, dried again completely, beaten with a cane and ironed with a warm iron over a sheet of paper. They would then look like new.

Many people felt that it was both uneconomic and inefficient to clean gloves at home, and preferred to send them to a professional cleaner. 'There are places, it seems, where, for twopence a pair, they are cleaned so as to look like new, and free from the offensive smell which used to distinguish this process,' remarks a mother of the 1850s to her daughter.[33] In fact, the cleaners mostly used the same processes and substances of the amateur, but in conditions of infinitely greater danger. 'The gloves . . . are scrubbed with a small brush, soap, and benzine; they are then rinsed in benzine and "made up". The Committee was informed that this has been carried on in kitchens and small rooms where cooking was going on at the same time, and in rooms above the ground floor, from which escape in case of fire would be sometimes impossible. . . . In one place, visited by the Committee, the girls in the glove-cleaning department told them that they had to come out for fresh air "pretty often", that the spirit got into their heads and made them "act silly".' [34]

Shoes and stockings were a far less potent status symbol than gloves, for the simple reason that they were very rarely seen. Gwen Raverat goes so far as to assert that 'legs had no value, except that of impropriety. This was the reason why quite well-dressed, but respectable, women did not seem to mind wearing shabby shoes and stockings.' The number of recipes for cleaning and restoring footwear throughout the period gives little support to this view, but certainly a lady was unlikely to be so readily condemned for inadequate shoes as for dirty gloves.

Shoes could be an expensive item in the budget, and the fact that they did not change in style at the same rate as other items of dress made it doubly imperative that they should last. 'If the new leather on soles of boots is well soaked for three days before use in linseed oil, to which a few drops of castor oil is added, and then allowed to stand for a few days to dry, it will last nearly twice as long.' [35] New boots were often difficult to polish, but if a little castor sugar was put on the brush for the final shine, this problem could be overcome; if they creaked, the soles were to be well soaped.

Many recipes were advocated for the waterproofing of boots and shoes. The soles might be varnished, or the whole shoe could be soaked for several hours in thick soap-water; it could be rubbed with a mixture of 'one part mutton suet and twice that quantity of beeswax, melted together', [36] left overnight, and polished with a piece of flannel in the morning. 'Although when the composition is first applied the leather will not polish as well as usual when blacked, yet they will be susceptible of a brilliant polish after the blacking has been applied a few times.' An equally good mixture consisted of beeswax, turpentine, Burgundy pitch and oil, melted together over a slow fire. If the housewife neglected to take these precautions, and her shoes became waterlogged and therefore liable to shrink and harden, she was advised to 'fill them with dry warm bran, and lace up tight, suspend in a warm place, not too near the fire, and you will find the bran will absorb all the moisture, and the leather will be soft and pliable, and not so likely to crack.' [37] Dry oats or paper could be substituted for the bran, and the shoes could be further softened by an application of glycerine, kerosene or vaseline. They might then be given a protective coat of varnish, made by dissolving 'half an ounce of asphaltum in one ounce of oil of turpentine, also dissolve quarter-of-an-ounce of caoutchouc in two ounces of mineral naptha. The two solutions are to be mixed before application.' [38] And if the boots were of the cloth variety with only a toe-cap of leather, and some of the varnish spilled over onto the cloth, then repeated applications of turpentine would rectify the damage.

Soiled shoes required more specialized treatment. The insides benefited from a fortnightly sponging with ammonia, which prevented offensive odours. The outsides, however, had to receive a treatment suited to their material. White satin shoes could either be rubbed with dry bread or wiped with spirits of wine, neither of which would damage the delicate fabric. Spirits of wine could also be used safely on white kid; alternatives were powdered starch or almond oil. Patent leather was treated with 'one pint of the best cream, one pint of linseed oil; make them each lukewarm and mix well together.' [39] Alternatively, if it had cracked, the cracks could be filled with blacking and then rubbed with French polish, ordinary furniture polish, or a mixture of sweet oil and turpentine, for 'the old plan of washing them with milk is simply absurd; a waste of time.' [40]

Leather could stand much harsher treatment than satin, kid or patent. Tan leather could be well cleaned by rubbing with the inside of a banana skin, while brown shoes responded well to 'two drachms of muriatic acid, the same quantity of spirits of lavender, and the juice of one lemon with half a pint of skimmed milk, in which half an ounce of gum arabic has been dissolved.' [41] Black boots and shoes could be rubbed with a slice of orange, or with black ink followed by salad oil, or with a home-made blacking. A typical recipe for this required spermaceti oil, treacle, powdered ivory black and vinegar; one even more improbable concoction consisted of 'one drachm of isinglass, half a drachm of indigo, half an ounce of soft soap, two ounces of glue, and a small handful of logwood raspings. Boil these all together slowly in one pint of vinegar, until the quantity is reduced one half.' This apparently produced 'a perfect shining jet . . . needing no brush, and making no dirt; nor will it soil the dress.'[42] Whichever method was preferred, it was advisable to follow it by an application of glycerine, which both softened the leather and protected the surface.

Socks and stockings required careful treatment if they were to retain their shape, texture and colour. Most people agreed that it was best to wash them at home, as laundresses had a bad habit of ironing them, which turned the white ones yellow, but numerous pitfalls awaited the inexperienced housewife, as one of them testifies. Determined to wash her husband's socks herself, she was nevertheless completely at a loss how to begin. 'I was dreadfully puzzled, and I would not lessen my dignity as the mistress of a household by getting information from Mary. So I watched her when she washed, and I did exactly the same as she did. Tom's socks were coloured ones, and woollen. Mary used soda, so did I, and took all the skin off my fingers and the colour from my socks. Mary boiled her clothes, so did I mine, and I wish you could have seen those three pairs of socks of my husband's, as Mary, with a horrified face, for I had popped them into the copper during her momentary absence, pulled them out and groaned, "Oh missus, them things oughtn't to be biled." '[43]

Silk stockings could be washed in soft water and Castile soap; they were to be squeezed rather than rubbed, stretched into shape and dried away from direct heat, then rubbed with a piece of soft flannel to bring up their lustre. A glass of gin could be added to the washing water, and the rinsing water could be tinged with a little blue or pink. The stockings could safely be mangled, provided they were first sewn down onto a sheet; alternatively they could be folded inside a piece of calico and beaten with a rolling pin. On no account were they to be ironed, unless they were first folded inside a thick cloth; a towel was not considered suitable as its pile would leave an imprint on the stockings. Delicate hosiery of all kinds was soaked in salt water or in a weak solution of alum before wearing, and vinegar was added to the washing water.

All coloured stockings were liable to fade, but the danger could be minimized by adding a tablespoonful of black pepper to the rinsing water. Sugar of lead was even more effective, but had to be used with extreme caution, being a strong poison. Black was the most difficult colour to wash, because the dye streaked very readily. Improvements were made during the course of the century, and by

1892 *Enquire Within* could assert that 'nothing looks worse than the rusty, white-black stockings of years gone by, after they had been a short time in use, but the blue-black colour of the new dyes gives them an excellent appearance.' Nevertheless, for most of the Victorian period great care had to be taken when washing black stockings. Some claimed that 'if black . . . stockings . . . [are] boiled for a few minutes in milk, the dye will not stain the skin;'[44] others insisted that it was necessary to 'take a quarter of a pound of soft soap, the same quantity of run honey, and a large wineglass full of gin; mix these until dissolved, in a quart or three pints of soft warm water.'[45] The stockings were to be washed in this mixture, rinsed twice in rain water, wrung, smoothed out, dried away from the sun and ironed with a cool iron on the wrong side. 'This recipe was given me by a lady's maid of much experience, who told me she had washed black silk stockings in this way for years, and that if carefully and quickly done they will retain their colour.'

For many poorer people, the time and the materials needed for these techniques put them way beyond their reach, and makeshift methods had to be resorted to. Thus socks and stockings were frequently cleaned by being put to stew in the oven. 'I was once in a very tidy cottage home at dinner time,' wrote Ruth Lamb in *The Girl's Own Paper*, 'when a little lassie brought in a baked rice pudding, cooked in a small back kitchen. The mother noticed a peculiar odour, as the steam arose from the dish, and said "Polly, the pudding has a queer smell." "Yes, mother," replied the child, "the stockings have boiled over on the oven shelf. But nothing went in the pudding for *it* was on the top, and the stocking pot was at the bottom." This was reassuring, but the soapy liquid having boiled over on the hot shelf had burned there, and raised sufficient steam and smoke to give the pudding an undoubted flavouring of essence of stewed stockings.'[46]

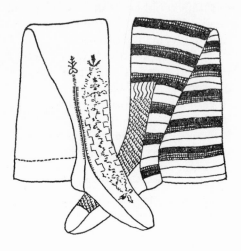

Lady's stockings of (l.) écru thread, (r.) striped cotton (1877)

Notes and References

1 *The Toilette,* 'by the Authors of "The Household Book of Practical Receipts" etc. etc.', 1854.

2 Anon., *Manners & Rules of Good Society,* 1888.

3 *The Ladies' Treasury,* 1857.

4 *How To Dress on £15 a Year, As a Lady,* op. cit.

5 Ibid.

6 *The Workwoman's Guide,* op. cit.

7 *The Toilette,* op. cit.

8 *Beauty: What It Is, and How to Retain It,* by a Lady, 1873.

9 *The Englishwoman's Domestic Magazine,* 1879.

10 *Beauty . . . ,* op. cit.

11 *Health, Beauty, & The Toilet,* by A Lady Doctor (Anna Kinsford M.D.), 1886.

12 *How To Dress Well on A Shilling A Day,* op. cit.

13 *Health, Beauty, & The Toilet,* op. cit.

14 Ibid.

15 *The Toilette,* op. cit.

16 Anon., *The Art of Dress,* 1839.

17 R. Fulford (ed.), *Dearest Child,* 1964.

18 *The Englishwoman's Domestic Magazine,* 1862.

19 *The Lancet,* quoted in *The Ladies' Treasury,* 1878.

20 *How To Dress on £15 a Year,* op. cit.

21 Ibid.

22 *The Englishwoman's Domestic Magazine,* 1879. A clock is a decorative pattern in openwork or embroidery worked up the side of a stocking.

23 *The Girl's Own Paper,* 1900.

24 *Miss Leslie's Magazine,* 1843.

25 *The Lady's Dressing-Room,* op. cit.

26 *The Ladies' Treasury,* 1857.

27 *Beauty . . . ,* op. cit.

28 *The Girl's Own Paper,* 1883.

29 *Cassell's Household Guide,* Vol. IV, op. cit.

30 *The Englishwoman's Domestic Magazine,* 1879.

31 *Home Notes,* 1894.

32 *Cassell's Household Guide,* Vol, IV, op. cit.

33 *The Ladies' Treasury,* 1857.

34 *Interim Report of the Departmental Committee appointed to Inquire into and Report upon certain Miscellaneous Trades* C8149, 1896, quoted in E. Royston Pike (ed.), *Human Documents of the Age of the Forsytes,* 1969.

35 *Home Notes,* 1894.

36 *Cassell's Household Guide,* Vol. IV, op. cit.

37 *Home Notes,* 1894.

38 *Cassell's Household Guide,* Vol. I, op. cit.

39 *Home Notes,* 1894.

40 *The Englishwoman's Domestic Magazine,* 1856-7.

41 *Cassell's Household Guide,* Vol. IV, op. cit.

42 *The Englishwoman's Domestic Magazine,* 1856.

43 *Sylvia's Home Journal,* 1878.

44 *Home Chat,* 1897.

45 *The Queen,* 1868.

46 *The Girl's Own Paper,* 1880.

6

Lace

The Victorians loved lace. It formed an indispensable trimming to numerous articles of dress, not infrequently it was made up into a complete garment, and because of its infinite yet subtle gradations of quality it could be used as a potent status symbol. Thus in Mrs Gaskell's *North and South,* when the two mothers first meet and appraise each other, 'Mrs Hale was making rather more exertion in her answers, captivated by some real old lace which Mrs Thornton wore; "lace", as she afterwards observed to Dixon, "of that old English point which has not been made for this seventy years, and which cannot be bought. It must have been an heir-loom, and shows that she had ancestors." '

Hand-made lace falls into two categories, needlepoint and bobbin lace. Needlepoint has the longer history, having evolved in the second half of the sixteenth century from the cut and drawn thread work which was popular in Italy at the time. It can easily be recognized by the fact that it is composed of tiny buttonhole stitches worked with a needle over a network of threads which forms the pattern. The designs are usually geometric. Needlepoint was much used as a dress trimming in the seventeenth century, and examples of it have always been highly prized, but it was never made to any great extent in England. Bobbin lace differs from needlepoint in that it is not worked by the needle; it is formed by the interweaving, plaiting and twisting of a number of threads, each one wound onto a bobbin, the work being pinned in position on a firmly stuffed cushion or pillow. By this means, patterns of an extreme elaboration and grace can be achieved in a variety of styles.

The making of bobbin lace appears to have been a flourishing trade in England by the beginning of the seventeenth century. It was centred around two areas, Honiton in Devonshire, and the East Midlands – Bedfordshire, Buckinghamshire and Northamptonshire – each area producing its own type of lace. The characteristic feature of Honiton lace is that the different motifs are each made separately, and then joined together either by a net mesh being worked in the gaps between them, or by needlemade bars, or, in the later phases of the industry, by being applied on to a piece of ready-worked net. East Midlands lace, on the other hand, has the motifs and the groundwork made all in one piece. Whatever the method used, however, making lace by hand is an extremely slow and laborious process, and the end product has always been regarded as a luxury item and commanded high prices.

During the second half of the eighteenth century, the commercial possibilities of making lace by machine became apparent. The first attempts made use of the already established stocking frame, and a lace made by this method was patented in 1764. The next big advance came ten years later when the warp frame was invented. For whereas the stocking frame could only produce variations on what was basically the technique of knitting, resulting in an elastic fabric liable to unravel because it was formed of one continuous thread, the warp frame used a series of vertical threads which could then be zigzagged together, resulting in a much stronger fabric which could be cut with impunity. Lace was being produced by this means by the end of the century.

The first half of the nineteenth century was a period of rapid progress for the machine-lace industry, and inventions succeeded one another at a prodigious rate. Heathcoat's hexagonal-mesh net, patented in 1808, was a momentous advance and effectively dealt the death-blow to the East Midlands industry, as it required only hand-embroidering to produce a cheap and passable lace. (Honiton survived because its individually-made motifs could be applied straight onto the machine-made net, the hybrid result being known as Honiton appliqué and enjoying great popularity.) The Pusher machine of 1812 was the most versatile yet, and by the 1840s was turning out good imitations of bobbin lace which needed no hand-finishing. Soon machines could be made to turn out spotted net, and even to outline the motifs of the pattern with a thicker thread. In short, 'almost every year presents some new adaptation of mechanism, some new order of processes, by which a pattern is produced that could before only result from the needle of the embroiderer.'[1] The modernists exulted. The Jury of the Great Exhibition of 1851 referred contemptuously to hand-made lace as 'the primitive method', and boasted that 'those who, from their sex and the form of their attire, have most concern with lace as a material for ornamental dress, are seldom in a condition to decide whether lace is in our own day made by machinery or by hand, or how far the two are combined.' The fashion magazines were equally enthusiastic: 'The Royal Mechlin Lace, both in the fineness and transparence of the ground, and the exquisite beauty of the patterns, may stand a comparison, to its advantage, with the foreign Mechlin, whilst the immense difference in its price, must be an object to ladies who wish to dress well and fashionable at a moderate expense.'[2] And moderate the expense was, thanks to the perfected machinery, for lace which had cost thirty shillings per square yard in 1815 could be had for threepence in 1851.

Thus at the beginning of our period the English bobbin lace industry was already in decline. Since it was practised chiefly by home-workers in rural districts, its organization had always been weak, and now it found itself quite unable to compete with Nottingham's 'lace of finer quality, more even in its texture, and considerably more elegant in its appearance than any bone-lace [i.e. bobbin lace] whatever, and at about one-third the price of bone-lace'.[3] The handful of people who were still prepared to pay for real lace were unlikely to patronize the rather unsophisticated products of the East Midlands, and although Queen Victoria patriotically ordered a Honiton lace wedding dress at a cost of £1,000, this could have little lasting effect on the industry. Mrs Bury Palliser records that in the middle years of the century the parchment patterns from which the traditional Honiton designs were taken were so little valued that they were boiled down to make glue. Lace generally was finding that it had little place in the new machine age, and a dismal picture of its situation is painted by the *Dictionary of Needlework* of 1882:

'The decline in the demand for so costly an article, added to the very small remuneration each lace worker could hope to receive for almost unremitting toil, the loss of eyesight entailed, the troubles in France and Holland (the principal places of its production), and the invention of the Bobbin net machine, and finally, of the lace making machine, have all contributed to the decay of this art, and now only such laces as Brussels, Lille, Mechlin, Valenciennes and Honiton are made to any amount, these by their beauty, intrinsic value, and merit, being still able to contend against all disadvantages, and obtain high prices; but for how long they can stand against the cheap and good machine imitations is a matter of doubt, and much fear is entertained that the delicate art of lace making will become extinct.'

Towards the end of the nineteenth century, attempts were made to inject new life into the moribund bobbin lace industry. Mrs Bury Palliser had published her monumental *History of Lace* in 1869; as a third edition was necessary by 1875, it must at least have revived interest in, and appreciation of, hand-made lace. In the 1890s various associations were formed by people concerned at the dying-out of a traditional art, and patrons attempted to improve the quality and saleability of hand-made lace, but their efforts were ultimately in vain, and if lace-making was continued at all it was by those with sufficient leisure and means to regard it as a pastime.

Throughout the Victorian period there was a constant demand for all types of lace, from the narrow edgings used on undergarments to lace 'in the piece' which could be made up into a whole dress. At the highest level, Honiton lace, or at least Honiton appliqué, became standard bridal wear for everyone who could afford it, Queen Victoria having set the fashion at her own wedding. Princess Alexandra, married in 1863, wore 'a petticoat of white satin covered with four flounces of the richest Honiton lace',[4] with a train and veil to match. When the less exalted Gertrude Vernon plans her wedding outfit in 1858, her mother suggests 'a rich white glace, flounced, and over the silk flounces, flounces of lace to correspond with that of your veil – Honiton, I recommend.'[5]

In the late 'thirties the craze for things Gothic was reflected in the lace fashions, and *The World of Fashion* for 1838 informs us that 'the trimming expected to be the most in request, is old-fashioned point lace. We may still call it antique, for the patterns now presented to our elegant fashionables, are those that were the mode centuries ago. . . . The most curious of all are those which

Pattern for a point lace collar (1869)

present us with armed knights in different attitudes.' Lace clearly
found its most versatile use as a trimming, and was used with in-
discriminate enthusiasm at this time, perhaps owing to its increasing cheapness: 'Lace is, in fact, an accessory to even the most
complete deshabille, and the distinction formerly made of having
different laces for different times of day seems to be in a great
measure abolished. It is true that Valenciennes continues to be as
it always hitherto has been, employed for undress or demi-toilet,
but antique point is used for the simplest deshabille, the elegant
half-dress, and the superb evening costume.'[6]

Lace flounces on dresses were extremely popular in the 'forties
and 'fifties, but lace was also used to make complete dresses. The
Victorians enjoyed contrasts of texture and colour in their clothes.
It is easy, when reading the innumerable references to black lace,
to imagine dark and dreary outfits, and it comes as a pleasant surprise to read that 'black lace dresses worn over rose coloured satin,
are also expected to be very fashionable.'[7] In the late 'fifties and
'sixties, when the crinoline had reached its zenith, the same
contrast was achieved by wearing black lace shawls, spread out to
their best advantage over the vast expanses of light-coloured skirt.

The fragility and delicacy of lace, which made it an ideal trimming for caps, bonnets and summer dresses, also rendered it suitable for small articles, and lace fans enjoyed great popularity from

the 1860s onwards. The most fashionable at this time had leaves of black Chantilly, though fans with a white leaf lined with the same fabric as the dress were also sought after. In the 'eighties and 'nineties the fashion turned to needlepoint, Honiton appliqué or Honiton guipure, a fan being the ideal way to show off a small piece of good lace.

Although Victorian fashion magazines refer constantly to lace, it is very seldom that they commit themselves as to type. True, they sometimes specify 'point', but it is clear that this word soon ceased to mean very much; 'as it has been applied to many laces that are only made on the pillow, and to laces that are made either by the hand or on the pillow, it cannot be looked upon as a perfectly correct indication of the nature of the lace.'[8] Clearly, while the wearing of lace was a matter of fashion, the type was left for the taste and purse of the wearer to decide.

For many people the attraction of cheap machine lace was further enhanced by the feeling that it was 'modern'. In Flora Thompson's Lark Rise of the 'eighties, where the rector's daughter loaned out christening robes to needy villagers, 'one woman ripped off the deep flounce of old Buckinghamshire lace from the second-best christening robe and substituted a frill of coarse, machine-made embroidery, saying she was not going to take her child to church "trigged out" in that old-fashioned trash. As she had not troubled to unpick the stitches, the lace was torn beyond repair, and the gown ever after was decidedly second-best, for the best one was the old Rectory family christening robe and made of the finest lawn, tucked and inserted all over with real Valenciennes.'

Most people, however, appreciated the difference between real and machine lace. For despite the boast of the Great Exhibition jury it *was* possible to tell them apart, and the real had reasserted its superiority in most circles. The true problem was one of cost. Writers on dress tackled this in different ways. The author of *How To Dress on £15 a Year* pleads that good lace is a sound investment: 'It makes the simplest bonnet look good and ladylike, and is as cheap, if not cheaper (in the long run) as imitation, for it will trim six or seven bonnets in succession, with care, and being heedful not to cut it unnecessarily.'[9] The author of *How To Dress Well on A Shilling A Day*, on the other hand, evades the issue by remarking complacently that 'some good old lace is an invaluable possession to a woman who has to dress inexpensively,'[10] a depressing statement for those without family heirlooms to fall back on. For women who had no lace to inherit and no money to buy new, the only solution was to make their own.

Even to the Victorians, who were accustomed to exacting needlework, the production of needlepoint or bobbin lace must have seemed a daunting task. Some brave souls no doubt ventured upon it, but the evidence of magazines and books of needlework is that most resorted to allied but less demanding forms of craft. The 'fifties and 'sixties saw a great vogue for tatting and crochet. Tatting was recommended as 'a sort of work that requires no sight, and which can be carried safely in the pocket, and taken out at any time. . . . It is among the most delightful resources for the delicate, and those whose sight is not strong. Besides, the work washes and wears forever.' [11] Although, because of its structure, tatting is particularly suitable for small collars, cuffs and edgings, it was also sometimes formed in the piece, judging by a panel for the front of a christening robe which has been preserved.

Crochet was another technique whereby lace-like trimmings could be produced at home. *The Young Ladies' Journal* of 1887 informs us that it 'was not popular work in England until c. 1840, when for quite twenty years it was very fashionable; and exceedingly beautiful designs, copies of Rose Point and Venetian lace were much worked. This more elaborate kind of crochet comes to England still in large quantities as Irish point.'

But the most popular of all these crafts was the so-called modern point lace. An example of this was shown at the Great Exhibition, where it won the praise of the jury for its 'delicate fairy-like texture'. Since the *Report* goes on to explain not only how the work was done but also where the materials could be had, we may assume that it was something of a novelty. It rapidly caught on, however, and ultimately ousted tatting as a popular pastime. It was made by tacking down a purpose-bought narrow tape onto a printed pattern, following all the outlines of the design; the gaps between the meanders of tape were then filled in with a variety of needlemade fillings, and when the work was completed it was cut away from the pattern. The result was heavy and coarse compared to genuine needlepoint, but it must have been satisfying to work, judging from its frequent appearance in magazines, and boldly effective to wear: 'The truth is, it is almost a waste of time to lavish too minute stitches on these patterns, because it is effect that is most aimed at, and lace is used in such liberal folds that any intricacies of detail are lost.'[12]

CARE AND CLEANING

The charm of lace lies as much in its characteristic textures and colours as in its design, and one careless wash is sufficient to ruin it forever. We have already seen that good lace was not easy to come by in the Victorian age. Clearly, whether she had preserved a grandmother's heirloom, like Mrs Thornton, blued her dress allowance, or spent hours with her needle or crochet hook, the Victorian housewife was going to take good care of her lace and make sure that it lasted.

As the fabric was far too delicate to withstand a normal wash, cleaning lace was a complicated process and the lady of the house was advised to superintend the work in person. She had first to equip herself with some lace-bottles and earthenware crocks. The bottles 'should be straight black bottles of the largest size, and it is well to buy them new for the purpose; otherwise something of their former contents may come out in boiling, and injure the lace; also there may be the remains of wax, rosin, or some other cement lingering about the place where the cork was; and this will melt in the water, and streak the lace. The bottles being perfectly clean, inside and out, cover them with coarse, strong, new white linen, sewed on tightly and smoothly with coarse thread. When not in use, keep them wrapped up in clean brown paper.' As for the crocks, 'an iron or tin vessel must on no account be used . . . or the lace will become black rather than white.' A porcelain kettle was suitable, but 'if the coating or lining . . . is in the least cracked or scaled off, do not boil the lace in it, or it will be stained with iron mould.'

The soiled lace was wound smoothly round the bottle from bottom to top, 'in such a manner as to leave the scolloped or pattern-edge visible all round', and the ends were secured to the bottle cover with a stitch or two. One of the crocks was filled with soft cold water, and the lace-bottle was put into it early in the evening and left to soak all night, though 'it will be well to change the water just before bed-time.' In the morning, the other crock was filled with a 'strong suds' of cold water and fine unscented white soap. 'Tie a twine string to the neck of the bottle, and make it fast round the handles or rim of the vessel, to keep it as steady as possible while boiling. As soon as the bottle, with the lace on it, has been put into the suds, set the vessel over hot coals, and keep it boiling steadily for an hour and a half.... When the lace looks very nice and white, take the bottle out of the kettle, turn it up to drain off the suds, and then set it (without rinsing) out in the sun. Keep it in the sun till the lace dries on the bottle. . . . Of course it should be done in fine weather, as it will not dry white by the fire. . . . Thread lace done exactly according to these directions, has the look, feel, transparence, and consistence of new lace that has never been washed at all; and is frequently mistaken for it. Drying in the soap-suds gives it just the right stiffness, and it will last much longer than if washed in the usual manner with squeezing, rinsing, starching, clapping and ironing.' [13]

Although the above instructions would apply to most laces, there was also an abundance of more specialized methods for the different types of lace. One of the most fragile was blonde, which was a lace made of silk. This could be soaked for half an hour in a solution of salts of tartar, squeezed out, and left to dry, but 'if valuable it is much the best to send it to a professional cleaner'.[14] Honiton was another valuable lace for which professional attention was sometimes advocated, but thrifty housewives were reluctant to pay out good money if there was any possibility of doing the job themselves: 'I should feel very much obliged if you or any of your readers could inform me how to clean Honiton lace veils as my milliner informs me that starch completely ruins them, and by giving them to her she charges me (for sending them away and cleaning) two shillings each, which I consider too much.'[15] The recommended technique was to 'cover a flat board with flannel, tack the lace evenly on to it, and cover with a piece of muslin (an old handkerchief will do). Wash the muslin with a soap lather, rubbing with the hand; this will soak through to the lace beneath. Rinse out two or three times with clean water, and allow it to dry on the board. Then remove it and pull the pattern out carefully with the fingers.' [16] If the lace was considered too delicate to be soaped, it could be pinned to a covered board and dabbed with benzine. 'For specially obstinate spots, lay on a bit of linen and pour on the benzine until it is soaking wet. Then press it down firmly against the lace, changing to a clean spot, as the dirt comes through the cloth. .... When the dirt is removed, take the lace from the board, lay it smoothly betwixt the folds of a towel, and put it in the sunshine for twelve hours, after which it will look like new and have no smell about it. This process is the best for very fine laces.'[17] Another, 'much less tedious' method was to rub the lace all over with soap and put it loosely into a glass container filled with soft water. This was then left for twelve hours in full sunlight, after which the lace was removed and rinsed without rubbing or squeezing.

The coarser varieties of lace could, of course, stand much rougher treatment, and tatting could be boiled in soapy water without even being attached to a bottle, but some of the very textured types might be impaired by wetting. For these some kind of dry-cleaning was necessary. Cream-coloured Spanish lace could simply be rubbed with flour and pinned out in a wind, the flour carrying the dirt with it as it was blown away. Point lace, if not too dirty, could be cleaned 'by fixing it in a tent or frame (like the frame of a slate, with calico or ribbon wound round the two ends to fasten the lace to), and rubbing it gently with bread with the crust pared off.[18] Macramé lace, which was made by knotting stout thread into a highly textured pattern, 'must never be washed. Spread it out on a clean cloth, and cover it thickly with equal parts of very dry breadcrumbs and oatmeal, mixed together. Rub this well over the lace, using a hard-bristled brush, and when the crumbs are dirty, shake them off. Repeat the process till the work looks clean.'[19]

Excessively white lace was not admired by the Victorians. On the whole a more creamy shade was considered preferable, and to achieve this the lace, after being washed, was treated. 'Everyone knows that washed lace is improved by being dyed in cold coffee, but perhaps blondes are not aware that if it be dipped in tea it will become a colour more likely to suit them. At any rate, lace dyed in tea is a nice change and keeps fresh longer.'[20] Alternative colouring agents were equal parts of beer and water, or an infusion of snuff. For a more yellowish tinge, the lace had to be dabbed here and there with olive oil before washing, and 'for very yellow lace, yellow ochre may be used for tinging the rinsing water. The ochre should be tied in a piece of flannel and used in the same way as the blue-bag.'[21]

Black lace required special attention because it was liable to discolour and go 'rusty'. Many of the cleaning agents were therefore colour fixatives as well, such as bullock's gall diluted with warm water, or an infusion of scalded bran. Alternatively the lace might be sponged with a solution of sal volatile, or of borax and spirits of wine, or it could simply be rinsed in milk, cold tea, or table-beer, the latter being particularly effective against mildew. Finally, if all else failed, 'rusty black lace may be renovated by dipping it in good black ink, wringing it in a cloth, and ironing it wet. This is rather a disagreeable process for the hands, but, if a little care and caution be observed, the fingers need scarcely come into contact with the ink. The lace can be stirred about with a stick, then pressed against the sides of the basin, and afterwards wrung out in an *old* cloth.'[22]

Washed lace might well end up rather limp, and require treatment to give it back some body. 'Starch in it is the abomination of desolation,'[23] so alternative stiffeners were found. A little gum-arabic might be dissolved in the washing water, or the lace might be dipped in a solution of white wax, white sugar and white soap, or wrung out in a 'soft liquid made by boiling a black kid glove in water until it is of the consistency of thin starch.'[24] 'Water in which a raw Irish potato has been grated is good for lace skirts, or anything where an enduring stiffness is requisite;'[25] the Honiton lace-makers, however, preferred water in which a little rice had been boiled. Tatting, because of its sturdy nature, was excepted from the general embargo on starch, while nets, at the opposite extreme, could only be stiffened by steaming.

Smoothing was the next problem to tackle. Ironing was considered 'little short of profanation',[26] as it ruined the texture and discoloured the lace. Steaming had a freshening effect, and in Honiton the lace was simply rubbed with a smooth piece of ivory, a substitute for which was 'an old-fashioned round topped silver pencil case . . . spreading the lace upon a hard cushion'.[27] Similarly it could be arranged between sheets of clean paper or cardboard and put under a weight. In all these cases it had first to be carefully pulled into shape with the fingers. If the lace was still damp from the wash, it could be wound carefully around a bottle previously filled with hot water, but the best, if also the most tedious, method was to 'put a clean cloth on the ironing-board, pin the lace in shape on it, a pin to each point.'[28] This might take a very long time, but it ensured that the lace dried in perfect shape.

A point lace fan (1876)

The lace was now, at last, clean, dry, smooth and stiffened. If it was not to be worn again immediately, great care had to be taken over its storage, or all the hard work would be undone. To prevent it from discolouring, it could be put in a box and heavily sprinkled with magnesia. This was particularly suitable for veils, for 'magnesia will remove the oily substance which gathers on lace after contact with the hair.'[29] Narrow strips of lace were wound round ribbon-blocks, which could be bought from ribbon shops: 'Wrap the block, with the lace on it, in soft *brown* paper, and put it away. If you have no ribbon-block you may roll up the lace round your fingers, and wrap it *lightly* in paper, taking care not to squeeze or press it.'[30] Brussels lace required very special treatment, as it was 'never washed after it is made, and is rubbed over with a white powder, which turns red if exposed too long to the air, or placed near a strong scent of any kind. In order to prevent injury to it, keep it carefully wrapped up in new silver paper, and place it in a tin box or a thick paper bag, turned over, and carefully sewed and stitched on something that will keep it in shape.'[31] The white powder was in fact lead carbonate, and highly poisonous.

It is easy to reach an academic assessment, from the foregoing information, of how much lace meant to the Victorian woman, but the knowledge is much more graphically brought alive in an episode from Mrs Gaskell's *Cranford* relating to 'some fine old lace, the sole relic of better days, which Lady Glenmire was admiring on Mrs Forrester's collar.' Mrs Forrester is recounting a 'narrow escape' which this lace once had:

'Of course, your ladyship knows that such lace must never be starched or ironed. Some people wash it in sugar and water, and some in coffee, to make it the right yellow colour; but I myself have a very good receipt for washing it in milk, which stiffens it enough, and gives it a very good creamy colour. Well, ma'am, I had tacked it together (and the beauty of this fine lace is that, when it is wet, it goes into a very little space), and put it to soak in milk, when, unfortunately, I left the room; on my return, I found pussy on the table, looking very like a thief, but gulping very uncomfortably, as if she was half-choked with something she wanted to swallow and could not. And, would you believe it? At first I pitied her, and said "Poor pussy! poor pussy!" till, all at once, I looked and saw the cup of milk empty – cleaned out! "You naughty cat!" said I, and I believe I was provoked enough to give her a slap, which did no good, but only helped the lace down – just as one slaps a choking child on the back. I could have cried, I was so vexed; but I determined I would not give the lace up without a struggle for it. I hoped the lace might disagree with her, at any rate; but it would have been too much for Job, if he had seen, as I did, that cat come in, quite placid and purring, not a quarter of an hour after, and almost expecting to be stroked. "No, pussy!" said I, "if you have any conscience you ought not to expect that!" And then a thought struck me; and I rang the bell for my maid, and sent her to Mr Hoggins, with my compliments, and would he be kind enough to lend me one of his top-boots for an hour? I did not think there was anything odd in the message; but Jenny said the young men in the surgery laughed as if they would be ill at my wanting a top-boot. When it came, Jenny and I put pussy in, with her forefeet straight down, so that they were fastened, and could not scratch, and we gave her a teaspoonful of currant-jelly in which (your ladyship must excuse me) I had mixed some tartar emetic. I shall never forget how anxious I was for the next half-hour. I took pussy to my own room, and spread a clean towel on the floor. I could have kissed her when she returned the lace to sight, very much as it had gone down. Jenny had boiling water ready, and we soaked it and soaked it, and spread it on a lavender-bush in the sun before I could touch it again, even to put it in milk. But now your ladyship would never guess that it had been in pussy's inside.'

Notes and References

1 *Reports by the Juries of the Great Exhibition*, 1851.
2 *The World of Fashion*, 1846.
3 Anon., *The Book of English Trades*, 1824.
4 *The Ladies' Treasury*, 1863.
5 Ibid., 1858.
6 *The World of Fashion*, 1840.
7 Ibid., 1841.
8 S. F. A. Caulfeild and Blanche S. Saward, *The Dictionary of Needlework*, 1882.
9 *How To Dress on £15 a Year*, op. cit.
10 *How To Dress Well on a Shilling A Day*, op. cit.
11 *The Englishwoman's Domestic Magazine*, 1856.
12 *The Queen*, 1899, quoted in Patricia Wardle, *Victorian Lace*, 1968.
13 *Miss Leslie's Magazine*, 1843.
14 *Enquire Within*, 1894.
15 *The Queen*, 1863.
16 Ibid., 1879.
17 *Enquire Within*, 1891.
18 *The Queen*, 1871.
19 Ibid., 1895.
20 *Home Chat*, 1895.
21 *The Girl's Own Paper*, 1899.
22 *The Englishwoman's Domestic Magazine*, 1862.
23 *Enquire Within*, 1891.
24 Ibid.
25 Ibid.
26 Ibid.
27 *The Queen*, 1863.
28 *Enquire Within*, 1891.
29 *Home Notes*, 1894.
30 *Miss Leslie's Magazine*, 1843.
31 *The Queen*, 1867.

7

Furs and Feathers

The use of furs and feathers in dress has a long history, going back to primitive times when man was primarily a hunter, and used the skins and plumage of his prey both to clothe and to adorn himself. As society gradually became more stable and structured, and increasing areas of land were appropriated for human use, the wild animals which had abounded everywhere became more scarce, and furs and feathers became luxury items reserved for the use of the rich. By the beginning of Queen Victoria's reign, however, new circumstances prevailed which enabled a far greater number of people to enjoy these luxuries than ever before.

Industrial Britain could not supply her fashionable world with any but the most humble domestic creatures such as rabbits and poultry, so that the overwhelming majority of skins and feathers had to be imported; however, owing partly to the growth of the Empire and partly to England's prominent position in world trade, an infinite variety of exotic material was available on reasonable terms. Thus in 1851 England was being supplied with, among other things, chinchilla from South America, mink and musquash from North America, squirrel from Russia, and ermine from Norway and Siberia, to say nothing of ostrich feathers from Egypt, Syria and South Africa, birds-of-paradise from the Manillas and marabout from Calcutta; the *Illustrated Exhibitor* could remark complacently that 'it is not a little curious to find the skin in which a wild Tartar colt once scampered over his native steppes serving, perhaps, as a paletot to some tranquil commercial gentleman economically travelling in an English second-class railway-carriage.'[1]

With such an abundance of furs to choose from, it is not surprising that fashion had different favourites at different times. At the beginning of the period, ermine, chinchilla and sable were firmly established in the lead, though ermine was soon relegated to the nursery. Sealskin advanced rapidly in popularity from the 1850s onwards. In 1889 Mrs Oscar Wilde noted that 'chinchilla, one of the most expensive of all the furs, is seldom seen now, but sable always keeps its popularity. Last year dyed fox was the fashion, and cheap imitations of it were everywhere to be seen. Another year it is Astrachan, another year sealskin.'[2] Two years later, 'sealskins seem to be abundant. . . . Beaver is also worn, and astrachan. Sable is for the rich only, judging from the jacket I was lately shown costing £900; but mink is a very good fur to replace it, and looks very handsome.'[3]

Because of its weight and warmth, fur is primarily suited to outdoor dress, and fur, or fur-trimmed, mantles and jackets were in vogue throughout the period, the winter weather providing an excuse for their reappearance year after year. Thus *The Ladies' Cabinet* for 1842 informs us that 'the increasing severity of the weather has brought furs more than ever into vogue: many mantles are lined with them, and a still greater number trimmed. We need hardly observe that those lined with fur are only to be seen in the first style of carriage-dress, for as the reigning fur is still sable, it is too costly for any but belles of large fortune.' Two winters later, the same magazine recommended 'a velvet mantle, or polonaise, trimmed with the best sable fur, or, perhaps, a cardinal composed of that fur only, wadded and lined with rich satin. . . . The cardinal, and also the trimming, may be of ermine.' The *Illustrated Exhibitor* enthused over the 'beautiful lustre of the seal-skin, dyed and undyed . . . shown to advantage in mantles, pardessus, children's dresses, bonnets, coats, and waistcoats – the latter invaluable for winter-wear, as a preservation against the bronchial complaints.' In 1860 Jane Welsh Carlyle was delighted with the gift of a sealskin pelisse, 'a luxury I long sighed for but, costing 20 gns, it had seemed hopeless.'[4] The sensation of 1872 was 'a sealskin jacket trimmed with otter or beaver',[5] but towards the end of the period fur was more widely used as a trimming than to make up a whole garment, and Harrods stocked fur trimmings in a variety of

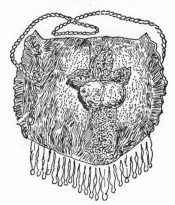

Young girl's sealskin hat and muff (1885)

qualities and widths. By 1891, 'fur trimmings to cloth jackets consist of high collar, cuffs, and bands of fur down the front, or wide
revers, which can be closed at pleasure, and handsome frogs of
ornamental passementerie buttoned over them. Dresses are also
much trimmed with bands of fur this winter round the plain skirts,
and on the bodice or coat.'[6]
Fur was also extensively used for muffs, which were carried
throughout the period. In the 'forties and 'fifties they consisted of
a cylinder about nine inches long, lined with silk and padded with
curled horsehair and wadding. Thereafter they shrank to the minimum size which would accommodate the hands, and remained
small for the next twenty years. It was in the 1880s that they
returned to prominence, with an increase in size and a profusion of
trimming, to such an extent that 'now-a-days even the poor little
"slavey" has her muff made of dyed rabbit-skin or cat's fur, and it
is merely a question of the length of the purse that decides what
fur is to be worn.'[7] The 'eighties also revived the 'forties' fashion
for cuffs to match the muff, and instituted the muff-bag, which
was a handbag with a separate compartment on the outside into
which the hands could be slipped.
The Lady's Newspaper noted in the Great Exhibition 'boots of
seal-skin, bordered with ermine, as pretty and becoming as they
are warm and comfortable',[8] but this novel use for fur does not
seem to have been followed up, and it is likely that these boots were

exhibition pieces only.

The *Illustrated Exhibitor* noted that 'the manufacture of feathers gives employment to a great number of females, and is principally confined to England and France.' Certainly the demand for feathers never slackened throughout the Victorian period; they were used to trim hats, bonnets, mantles and parasols, and were made up into muffs and fans. Almost every year the magazines announce that 'feathers are a general trimming,' or 'feathers are the favourite ornaments for bonnets.' At the beginning of the period, birds-of-paradise were among the most popular; *The Ladies' Cabinet* for 1844 informs us that 'birds-of-paradise, with their beautiful plumage, in its natural state, others dyed to correspond with the chapeau, ostrich and willow plumes, marabouts, and fancy feathers; the latter, in the greatest possible variety, are all employed.' In the second half of the century, ostrich feathers gained the lead. The birds were extensively farmed, notably in South Africa, and the feathers imported in such quantities that soon even the little servant girls of Flora Thompson's Lark Rise had their 'best hats with the red roses and ostrich tips'. *The Woman's World* announced in 1889 that 'ostrich feathers have probably never been so much worn as they will be this winter. There will be feather boas and feather muffs, and no hat will be considered well trimmed that does not display a profusion of plumes of sufficient length to allow the tips to curl over the brim and nestle upon the hair.' Feather boas had the disadvantage that 'even the expensive ones shed their feathers so dreadfully that they are soon spoilt. Those of curled feathers have been immensely popular by reason of their becomingness . . . but they are the worst of all in point of wear.'[9] Despite this drawback, boas continued to enjoy a popularity which alarmed the more exclusive: 'There is some fear that these extremely pretty things are becoming common. Sales, alas! and the tremendous overstocking of the articles, have brought them down to popular prices, and they are no longer so chic. But still, the possessor of a really good feather boa need never despair, for its extremely softening effect is ever desirable.'[10] Fans were another favourite use for feathers, and the height of fashion in 1887 was a fan composed of 'about 16 magnificent ostrich feathers mounted in tortoiseshell, with monogram, coronet, or a spray of brilliants, apparent on the outside of the frame. Needless to say that the price of these insures to them a certain degree

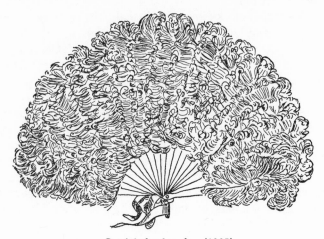

Ostrich-feather fan (1895)

of exclusiveness.'[11]

In the 1880s the general taste for furs and feathers took a particularly gruesome turn, and it became the fashion to wear clothes trimmed with whole animals or birds. Thus *The Ladies' Treasury*, describing an illustration of a Promenade Dress in 1883, remarks serenely: 'The artificial cat secures the folds of the tunic on the right side;' the hat belonging to the outfit is trimmed with a cockade of ribbon and a cat's head. Other hat trimmings included 'a seagull, a tiny nest containing the daintiest of ouistitis [a small monkey], with its tail turned up into an aigrette',[12] and we read

Aigrette of tinted feathers (1888)

that in 1884 'exotic birds are as much sought after as ever; they are placed in little nests of tulle and gauze upon the front of a low bodice, or by way of bouquet upon a short sleeve.' [13] However, the magazines retained an ambivalent attitude to these extravaganzas. The same one which had approved the stuffed cat had nothing but scorn for a lady who wore a hat composed of a single bird, while other birds were embroidered over her dress and yet another perched on her parasol – presumably even in this fashion there was such a thing as excess; other magazines were still more severe, *The Young Ladies' Journal* stating emphatically that 'to be well dressed it is not necessary to adopt all the vagaries of fashion and to wear cats' heads, tiny monkeys, and large parroquets upon one's bonnets, as I am sorry to say some Parisian ladies are doing,' and *The Girl's Own Paper* referring with distaste to 'any amount of the most horrid things of Parisian origin, the last being a small kitten – not real, I am glad to say, only an excellent imitation.' Thus the English people who found the fashion repugnant abnegated all responsibility for it, laying the blame squarely at the door of the French.

Inevitably a reaction set in, on grounds both of hygiene and of humanitarianism. The 1880s saw a very general concern for hygiene, its chief exponent being Dr Jaeger, who stressed the importance of healthy perspiration. His ideas gained wide acceptance; thus in *Health, Beauty, & the Toilet* 'A Lady Doctor' condemns the use of animal hides in dress because 'stripped from the carcase, and having undergone an astringent and hardening process, called "tanning", [they] have lost their permeability, they no longer admit ventilation, and, if worn as clothing, they tend to repress transpiration, and to shut in beneath them the exhalations of the body, which, consequently, condense as perspiration on the surface of the skin, and render it clammy and unclean.' But humanitarianism was also gaining ground, and the same author continues: 'Moreover, the fur trade, and especially that branch of it known as the seal fishery, involves very great cruelty, and this consideration ought not to pass for nothing with good women. There are few worse barbarities in the world than those which are perpetrated in the Arctic seas on the gentle and intelligent seals. . . . When they first came to my knowledge, I had a seal dolman in my wardrobe, but I could never put it on again afterwards; so I got rid of it at the first opportunity, and have never bought a strip of fur of any kind since.'

Feathers were not considered unhygienic, because they were very light to wear and were attached to a cloth backing which allowed for ventilation. Their use was attacked, however, by humanitarians. Whether ostrich feathers could be gained without pain to the bird was never finally established. Many people believed that the feathers were not pulled out but merely clipped, and therefore felt justified in wearing them. A first-hand observer reported that both methods were in use, adding that pulled feathers were considered finer than clipped ones, and shelving the cruelty problem by concluding airily: 'It is safe to affirm that this gives no pain to the birds, as the new feathers commence to grow again immediately.' [14] At any rate public feeling was not initially concerned with the ostrich, but with the scores of other birds which were actually slaughtered to provide hat trimmings. As early as 1884, *The Girl's Own Paper* was exclaiming: 'I only wish every girl or woman would avoid using dead birds at all in her dress; it seems such a needless cruelty towards God's beautiful creatures.' Five years later a positive step forward was taken with the founding of the Society for the Preservation of Birds. Its aim was to 'discourage the enormous sacrifice of bird-life at present exacted by the milliners', and its members had to undertake 'that they will refrain from wearing the feathers of any bird that is not killed for purposes of food, the ostrich only excepted.' [15] The range of birds exploited by the millinery trade is illustrated by a satirical poem in *Punch*:

> Hang me, Ladies fair, if tell I can
> Why you'd slay the blameless pelican,
> Or to utilise slang lingo –
> 'Spifflicate' the poor flamingo,
> Give the 'adjutant' his gruel,
> And, with faces blandly cruel,
> Cause the stork, the crane, the gannet,
> To skedaddle from our planet,
> Like the dodo, prematurely,
> Just to deck your bonnets! Surely
> In pursuit of Fashion-culture
> To kill out the useful vulture,
> Or exterminate the eagle
> Bird (excuse the rhyme) so regal

Rob, as it is feared your manner is,
Of its snowy plumes our swanneries;
Needlessly 'wipe out' macaws,
And, without sufficient cause,
Lessen, as by annual inches,
Our supplies of tits and finches,
Surely all this ruthless slaughter
Means disgrace to each Eve's daughter.

Despite their occasional complaints, the fashion magazines did not really feel at home among humanitarian arguments; their business was to condemn fashions that were no longer fashionable, rather than to concern themselves with ethics. Thus *The Lady's World* announced that 'the woman who appears in the dress-circles at a theatre with a swallow-shaped bird in flamingo colours laid upon the flattened surface of her head, advances an argument for their discontinuance infinitely more eloquent than any put forth by the Selborne Society.' And indeed the fashion did burn itself out in time, as all extreme fashions do; whole seagulls and kittens were discarded, and there was a return to more discreet furs and feathers.

Really good furs commanded exorbitant prices. It is not surprising to hear, therefore, that there was a brisk market in fakes. At the Great Exhibition, 'Messrs Robert Clarke and Son, generously willing to afford us that instruction which shall in future enable us more easily to distinguish the real from the false, have exhibited ... some specimens of a fur called "Musquash", the fur, we believe, of the musk cat, which being dressed and dyed, is frequently sold for sable, when it is not a tithe the value, and of no durability. ... To show the extent of the deception it is only necessary to mention that a boa of this stuff, which will very soon lose even the small resemblance it bears to sable, is worth about 7s 6d, while a sable one might range from 5 to 50 guineas.'[16] Perkins, in his *Haberdashery and Hosiery*, remarks that all furs can be imitated more or less successfully, with the exception of ermine and chinchilla, which might explain why these two furs were so popular among the elite.

Fakes were perpetrated for other reasons than profit. For the fashion-conscious but impecunious Victorian girl, furs and feathers were a major problem. If she turned in desperation to *How To*

Dress Well on A Shilling A Day, she got no help, for the author states frankly: 'I have said nothing about furs, for if they are not already in the wardrobe, they will never be there till we have more to dress upon than 1s a day.' The only glimmer of hope was a generous husband: 'A muff is to the majority of Englishwomen almost a necessity, but I have not allowed for one in our list, concluding that monsieur le mari sometimes brings home a little cadeau to help out the 1s a day. If he objects to that on principle (some very unpleasant people do!) the muff, if indispensable, must be bought out of the savings.' The girl who was not blessed with either generous relatives or savings had to fall back on her own resourcefulness, but even for her there were possibilities. In 1838, when ermine was the most fashionable fur, the anonymous author of *The Work-woman's Guide* suggested that it could easily be imitated by sewing 'tails of false black sable into white Spanish rabbit skin, cut a little V and let the tail in, covering it over with the flap, and sewing the tail firmly in.' Later in the period, as technology advanced, artificial furs began to appear on the market, and 'for those who cannot afford real astrachan, there is the woven astrachan, which is an excellent imitation of the genuine fur, and is dyed in all colours, as well as in the orthodox black and grey.'[17] Patents for similar fabrics were taken out in 1842 and 1852; they consisted of a background material on which a pile was produced by 'little tufts of llama wool, sheep's wool, goat's hair, or other like material.'[18]

Feathers demanded a much smaller initial outlay, but the cost of their upkeep could be great. 'I would not advise anyone who has to be strictly economical to invest in feathers, unless she can curl them herself. Our climate is a foe to feathers, and paying to have them curled every few weeks makes them expensive eventually, even if the first cost be not very much.'[19] However, other sources could be tapped: 'for instance, if you keep poultry, the breast of a white Brahma, carefully skinned (it does not improve its appearance at table, but that will not matter), and afterwards rubbed with salt and pepper, and dried in the sun or in an oven, will, if mounted carefully, make as pretty a plume as you could wish, especially if you rob the cock as well of some of his black tail-feathers to form an aigrette: you need not pull them out, that would hurt him, but just cut them off, leaving an inch of root; if you do this in the summer, just before his moulting, he will not long have to show himself with a dishevelled tail. As to the mounting, that is an easy affair; it only requires a small piece of Persian silk, black or white, to match the feathers, and a handful of cotton wool or wadding to stuff it with, and make it set out nice.'[20]

Across the Atlantic, the heroine of Dorothy Canfield's *The Bent Twig,* beautiful but penniless, adopted the same plan when invited to a skating party: 'Furthermore, her costume prepared for this event . . . was one of her successes. It had been a pale cream broadcloth of the finest texture, one of Aunt Victoria's reception gowns, which had evidently been spoiled by having coffee spilled down the front breadth. Sylvia had had the bold notion of dyeing it scarlet and making it over with bands of black plush (the best bits from an outworn coat of her mother's). On her gleaming red-brown hair she had perched a little red cap with a small black wing on either side (one of Lawrence's pet chickens furnished this), and she carried the muff which belonged to her best set of furs. Thus equipped, she looked like some impish, slender young Brunhilde, with her two upspringing wings. The young men gazed at her with the most unconcealed delight.'

Aigrette of tinted feathers (1888)

CARE AND CLEANING

Furs and feathers were regarded as an investment, and expected to last for years. But they had to be looked after. Furs were principally susceptible to moth, but 'another cause of the decay of furs is the moisture to which they are frequently exposed; the delicate structure of the fine underfur cannot be preserved when any dampness is allowed to remain in the skin.' [21] There was also, of course, the simple problem of dirt. Various recipes were advocated for the cleaning of furs, but all were in principle the same. 'The following is the way in which furs are cleaned in that land of furs, Russia: Rye flour is placed in a pot and heated upon a stove, with constant stirring as long as the hand can bear the heat. The flour is then spread over the fur and rubbed into it. After this the fur is brushed with a very clean brush, or better, is gently beaten until all the flour is removed. The fur thus treated resumes its natural lustre and appears as if absolutely new.' [22] Hot sand was an alternative to hot flour, and other version recommended applications of wet bran followed by dry bran. 'The wet bran should be put on with flannel, and the dry with a piece of book muslin. Lastly, rub the fur thoroughly with magnesia on a piece of book muslin. The rubbing should be done against the grain of the fur.' [23] There were also professional cleaners for the faint-hearted.

When fur got wet, 'it should not be wiped, but only shaken, and laid in the sun or a warm room till dry.' [24] Alternatively it could be gently combed, 'taking care not to scratch the skin, and to separate the fur of any spots matted by rain; wipe them with a soft cambric handkerchief, and then brush them with a long haired milliner's brush.' [25] Whatever the method used, 'do not on any account hang it near a fire.' [26]

When it came to laying furs away for the summer, the greatest care had to be taken to preserve them from moth. Powdered borax, strong black pepper, hops, Russia leather and 'a piece of mould candle' were all considered good preservatives, but all had to be used in conjunction with stout linen or holland storage bags, and preferably an airtight box as well. 'I have preserved a handsome sealskin trimmed with fox in the following manner: I first powdered two or three ounces of camphor and sprinkled the jacket well with this, and then placed the sealskin in tissue paper, and out-

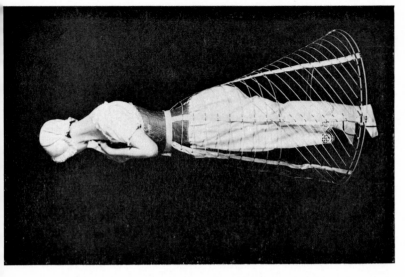

7 Model in underwear of the late 1860s: nightcap, chemise, corset, drawers and cage crinoline.

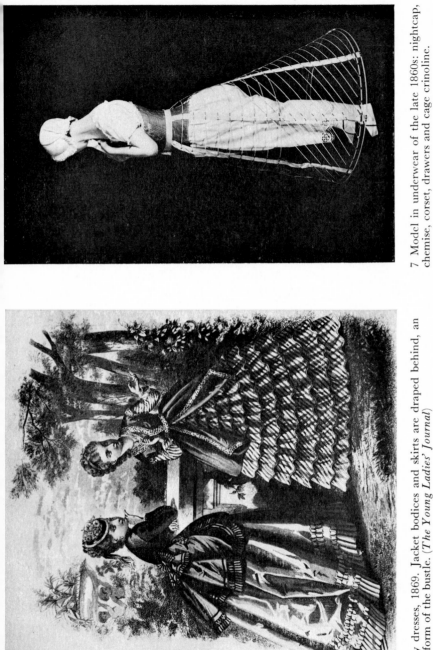

6 Day dresses, 1869. Jacket bodices and skirts are draped behind, an early form of the bustle. (*The Young Ladies' Journal*)

9 Outdoor dresses, 1887. Long bodices, angular bustles and tall hats produce a striking silhouette. (*The Ladies' Treasury*)

Le Monde Élégant

8 Evening dresses, 1877. Cuirasse bodices mould the figure; trimmings are pleated, ruched and flounced.

side brown paper, which I firmly stitched all round. Then I again well sprinkled with camphor, and placed in a trunk which is kept locked. The other day I took the sealskin out to see how this had answered, and the jacket was entirely free from moths. It has been put away all the summer and spring.' [27] A more drastic measure involved 'washing the skin with a solution of corrosive sublimate in as much spirits of wine as will dissolve it, and gently shaking it, dry near but not close to a fire. After this process has been gone through, the moth will not touch it, but it requires care, as corrosive sublimate is a strong poison.' [28] All these methods required that the fur be exposed to the air and well shaken once or twice during the summer period. If they all failed, and moth got into the fur, then the only remedy was to 'put it in a stove hot enough to bear the hand'.[29]

The simplest way to clean feathers was to wash them in a solution of white soap in soft water, with perhaps the addition of a small piece of pearl-ash. They could then be rinsed in cold water or rubbed through clean white paper. A more complex procedure was recommended for light feathers, and particularly grebe. 'Take a piece of clean old flannel, and well rub it with spirits of turpentine the way of the feathers, going twice over any part that may be very dirty until it looks a dull yellow. Have ready a tea tray or shallow box covered about an inch in depth with Plaster of Paris. Lay the grebe on this feather downwards, and completely cover it with more Plaster of Paris. Leave it from thirty-six hours to a week, remembering the longer it lies the whiter it will become. The Plaster of Paris can be saved, as it will do several times.' [30]

Cleaned feathers, or those which had been caught in the rain, became rather limp, and therefore had to be re-curled. The simplest way was just to shake them in front of a fire, and hope that they would re-curl naturally; but some people preferred to curl them over a 'small ivory paper-knife, or even a knitting needle, but I cannot help thinking that nothing answers so well for the purpose as the back of a penknife.' [31] However, others argued that 'a smooth piece of whalebone is better than a knife, for, having a less keen edge, it is not so liable to injure the feather.' [32]

Notes and References

1   *The Illustrated Exhibitor* (catalogue of the Great Exhibition), 1851.
2   *The Woman's World*, 1889.
3   *The Girl's Own Paper*, 1891.
4   J. A. Froude (ed.), *The Letters of Jane Welsh Carlyle*, 1883.
5   *The Queen*, 1872.
6   *The Girl's Own Paper*, 1891.
7   *The Woman's World*, 1889.
8   *The Lady's Newspaper*, 1851.
9   *The Girl's Own Paper*, 1891.
10 *The Lady's Realm*, 1898.
11 *The Lady's World*, 1887.
12 *The Young Ladies' Journal*, 1884.
13 Ibid.
14 *Sylvia's Home Journal*, 1885.
15 Reported in *Punch*, October 1889.
16 *The Lady's Newspaper*, 1851.
17 *The Girl's Own Paper*, 1884.
18 *Abridgements of Specifications relating to Wearing Apparel*, 1671-1866.
19 *How to Dress Well on A Shilling A Day*, op. cit.
20 *How To Dress on £15 a Year, As a Lady*, op. cit.
21 *Reports by the Juries of the Great Exhibition*, op. cit.
22 *Enquire Within*, 1892.
23 Ibid., 1894.
24 *The Workwoman's Guide*, op. cit.
25 *The Queen*, 1871.
26 *The Girl's Own Paper*, 1883.
27 *Enquire Within*, 1893.
28 *The Workwoman's Guide*, op. cit.
29 Ibid.
30 *The Queen*, 1867.
31 Ibid.
32 *Home Notes*, 1895.

8

Men's Clothes

Men's clothes changed relatively little during the sixty-four years of Victoria's reign. It is true that their cut and construction showed a certain amount of variation, but while women's clothes ran through a dazzling succession of styles, fabrics and colours, men retained the same basic garments, the same colours and fabrics, and approximately the same outline. A coat, waistcoat and trousers, not necessarily matching, and a white shirt, were worn throughout the period. The coat and trousers, and increasingly the waistcoat, were usually made of a woollen cloth, and the shirt, which had above all to be washable, was always of linen or cotton. Nor did the colours vary: a study of the fashion plates of the 'forties and 'fifties shows a predominance of black and dark blue, with occasional ventures into brown and green, while *Complete Etiquette for Gentlemen,* published in about 1880, remarks that 'the four staple colours for men's wear are black, blue, brown, and olive.'

It would be tedious painstakingly to examine the changes of cut that men's clothes underwent during Victoria's reign, cataloguing the number of buttons from year to year, and noting the comparative heights of collar or shapes of lapels. It is more interesting, after a quick look at their development, to try to understand the assumptions that underlay them, for in their unwavering sobriety they represent a unique phase in the history of fashion.

Broadly then, men's clothes changed from being colourful and still fairly exuberant in the first few years of the period, to become increasingly functional on the one hand, and sober on the other. This had two effects: one was an increase in comfort and informality, a rejection of elegance and its tyranny, and the other, following on from this, was a suspicion of anything ostentatious or effeminate. The fashionable ideal of the 1830s, as portrayed in the magazines, was a florid-complexioned youth, his chest and hips padded out on either side of his nipped-in waist – 'Fashion has moulded his body into a shape not unlike that of an ant'[1] – while by the 1850s, though the chest is still padded, the face is expressive of a clear-eyed integrity, and by the end of the period the stance is assertive and the expression stern.

Jane Welsh Carlyle, writing in 1845, records the change in the dress of one of the most notable dandies of the day: 'Count d'Orsay walked in. I had not seen him for 4 or 5 years. Last time he was as gay in his colours as a humming bird – blue satin cravat, blue velvet waistcoat, cream-coloured coat, lined with velvet of the same hue, trousers also of a bright colour, I forget what; white French gloves, two glorious breast pins attached by a chain, and length enough of gold watch guard to have hanged himself in. Today in compliment to his five more years, he was all in black and brown – a black satin cravat, a brown velvet waistcoat, a brown coat, some shades darker than the waistcoat, lined with velvet of its own shade, and almost black trousers, one breast pin, a large pear-shaped pearl set into a little cup of diamonds, and only one fold of gold chain round his neck, tucked right on the centre of his spacious breast with one magnificent turquoise.'[2]

Jane Welsh Carlyle attributes this altered appearance to d'Orsay's awareness of his increasing age, but the process was a more general one, and everywhere people were gradually changing to less remarkable attire. By the end of our period the two aspirations, to comfort and to manliness, were at their strongest. In 1896 the *Tailor and Cutter* published pictures of the latest fashions in France, Germany, America and England, with a view to comparing them. Not surprisingly, the foreign styles all come in for a good deal of criticism. The French are found guilty of 'a touch of effeminacy and love of pleasure', the Germans of excessive stiffness, and the Americans of being 'loud and elaborate', while in the English fashions can apparently be seen 'the easy good nature of John Bull. . . . There is an absence of military stiffness on the one hand, and luxurious effeminacy on the other' – in other words of the two things which had come to spell anathema to the Victorian man.

Taken year by year, the process was so slow as to be almost imperceptible. Trousers, for instance, changed very little during the whole period. For most of the time they were narrow, their smooth fit being ensured in the 'forties and early 'fifties by a strap under the foot. 'The best cut trowsers are always subject to a displacing of the seams, and it is only with straps they can be held in their proper position.'[3] From the late 'fifties to the mid 'sixties there was a fashion for so-called 'peg-top' trousers, that is to say trousers cut very full at the top and tapering sharply to the ankle. This mode was revived at the beginning of the 'nineties and lasted for most of that decade. With this exception trouser legs were straight, and the only other innovation was recorded by the *Tailor and Cutter* in 1895: 'Trousers have not varied much in shape or material, but we all must have noticed the revival of the crease down the centre of the leg.' For the early part of the period, day trousers were usually pale, and often checked or striped, but by the 'seventies the checks had become more discreet, and by 1880 pale trousers were for summer wear only. Black trousers were standard evening wear throughout the period.

At the beginning of the period the coat was a frock buttoning all the way down the front, with a low, nipped-in waist, a padded chest and a short skirt. In the 1850s it was replaced by the morning coat, which was less obviously waisted, with fronts curving away to the tail. The tail-coat proper was worn on formal occasions from the beginning of the period, but after the 'sixties it was evening wear only. The other coat forms of the period all show the trend towards comfort and informality. Two forms emerged in the 'sixties: a straight, short jacket with external pockets, which in its belted form was known as the Norfolk jacket, and a three-piece suit all of one fabric which evolved into the lounge suit. In addition the 1880s saw the appearance of the dinner jacket, informal in its shortness but reminiscent of the tail-coat by its roll collar; this grew rapidly in popularity, to the dismay of *The London Tailor*, which remarked in 1898 that 'it is an error for gentlemen to go to public dinners or to assemblies where ladies are present, in dinner jackets; and yet they will do it.'

For the first part of the period day waistcoats were ornate. The waistcoat was the last garment to lose its exotic character, and

Pattern for a gentleman's
embroidered waistcoat (1849)

during the 'forties and 'fifties devoted wives and sisters found in it a
vehicle for their most lavish embroidery. The magazines are full of
patterns for such colourful combinations as 'blue or claret velvet
or cloth, and green or amber Russia braid'.[4] Other waistcoats had
printed or woven designs. Evening waistcoats were somewhat
plainer; in 1843, in his *Practical Guide for the Tailor's Cutting-
Room,* Joseph Couts, while laying down black satin or white Mar-
seilles quilting, added witheringly: 'Now and then, it is true, a
vandalic incursion of fancy cut and flowered velvets and silk, with
gold and silver tissue woven into the pattern, may be seen, but rest
assured that the wearers, like their vests, are more showy than
tasteful.' After the 1860s the higher fastening of coats and the
fashion for matching suits resulted in the demise of the fancy
waistcoat.

The degree to which the shirt was visible varied according to the cut of the waistcoat, but it was always white, coloured shirts being unacceptable until the beginning of our own century. The author of *Complete Etiquette for Gentlemen* remarks sternly that 'figures and stripes do not conceal impurity, nor should this be a desideratum with any decent man.' The degree of starch on shirt fronts, collars and cuffs increased from the late 'sixties as clothes became more sombre, and the soft fronted shirt did not return until the 'nineties, when it accompanied the lounge suit. In 1895 the *Tailor and Cutter* referred with approval to 'the emancipation of man from the recent bullet-proof plaster of starch and stiffening known as a shirt front'.

One reason for the increasing sombreness of men's dress may perhaps be that the Victorian age was effectively ruled by the middle class, who differed from any previous ruling class in that they earned their living by commerce. The commercial world depends for its survival on a degree of professional integrity, 'the preservation of order and the sanctity of contracts'. Thus a psychologist like Dr Flügel asserts that 'in the thickness of material and solidity of structure of their tailored garments, in the heavy and sober blackness of their shoes, in the virgin whiteness and starched stiffness of their collars and of their shirt-fronts, men exhibit to the outer world their would-be strength, steadfastness, and immunity from frivolous distraction.'[5] And certainly the young Disraeli, making his way in the legal world, inspired little confidence with his 'green velvet trousers, a canary coloured waistcoat, low shoes, silver buckles, lace at his wrists';[6] he was known as 'that damned bumptious Jew boy' and was not considered a sound investment. That the Victorian man aimed at looking earnest and dependable is evidenced by this extract from an essay quoted in the *Tailor and Cutter* in 1871: 'The success of a commercial life, or a political career, depends, to a great extent, on the facility with which good impressions can be made on strangers. . . . No man who is interested in extending his influence can afford to be indifferent to his appearance. He may err by attiring himself too gaudily, as well as make a mistake by not dressing sufficiently well. . . . Carelessness and a want of neatness in personage, invariably indicate an entire lack of that methodical exactness so essential to the accomplishment of all pursuits in life. While on the other hand, a display of order and taste is a pledge that these excellent qualities extend to business transactions and penetrate the manners. . . . A gay or loud style

will as surely give an impression of emptiness and want of relia-
bility. . . .'

Thus the Victorian man sought above all to be inconspicuous,
offending nobody by anything extreme. The *Tailor and Cutter* laid
down in 1871 that 'material, colour and make-up should so perfectly accord that the outfit be utterly devoid of conspicuousness,
and taste and elegance be in such proportions of parts to each
other, that neither can be particularized, but present that pleasing
commingling so perceptible in all of nature's works,' and ten years
later *Complete Etiquette for Gentlemen* reiterated it: 'As in all
similar matters, it is the best taste not to deviate so much from the
prevailing modes as to make one's self remarkable.' How fashion
was ever supposed to change at all in this situation remains a
mystery.

Some men, of course, rejected this approach to dress completely.
Oscar Wilde remarked idealistically in 1882 that 'perhaps one of
the most difficult things for us to do is to choose a notable and joy-
ous dress for men. There would be more joy in life if we were to
accustom ourselves to use all the beautiful colours we can in fash-
ioning our own clothes.'[7] His own style of dress, nothing if not
conspicuous, was imitated by few and jeered at by many. In 1897
the *Tailor and Cutter* printed an article in which prominent artists
were asked their opinion of contemporary menswear. G. F. Watts
dwelt on the 'most ignoble character, alike in form, colour, and
material of modern costume.' Walter Crane observed that it was
'neither useful nor ornamental. Take it as a whole, the effect is
prosaic, tame, and uninteresting to a degree – neatness is about the
only one virtue or quality it may claim.' E. Onslow Ford thought
that 'the present style of dress that men are obliged to wear has
scarcely a redeeming feature.'[8] Interestingly enough, however,
most of them made an exception for sporting costume, which they
commended for being functional and comfortable, and in Walter
Crane's words, 'more or less picturesque because expressive and
adapted to the movements and contours of the body'. It took half
a century and two World Wars for their wishes to be realized, but
surely they would have approved of today's eminently practical
and workmanlike denims.

CARE AND CLEANING

The Victorian housewife was caused far less trouble by her husband's clothes than by her own. Here were no problems of fugitive dyes, limp feathers or yellowing lace. The basic rules were simple, if adamant: whites must be white, and blacks black. Shirts were laundered in the same way as the rest of the family underwear: it was their ironing and starching that required special attention and, judging from the number of enquiries in magazines on this subject, most bewildered and daunted the young bride. First of all, the starch had to be mixed with a suitable substance or substances, as used on its own it would impart stiffness but no shine. This much sought-after glossiness had a practical purpose in that it prevented dirt from adhering to the surface; thus at the end of a little story demonstrating the virtues of an understanding of laundry work, we are told that 'instead of needing a clean pair of cuffs every day, Mr Bowen wore his new ones with the "china facings" for several consecutive ones.'[9] Various additives were advocated, such as 'a very small piece of solid paraffin',[10] or a solution of borax mixed with either half a cup of milk or an ounce of white wax. A more ambitious preparation demanded 'spermaceti, a quarter of an ounce; gum, a quarter of an ounce; borax, half an ounce; glycerine, one ounce; water, ten ounces; mix thoroughly to a smooth cream, and use three teaspoonsful to a quarter pint of starch.'[11] Yet another alternative was 'a bit of white wax half the size of a small hazel-nut, and a teaspoonful of brandy. The spirit is to retain the stiffness and increase it, the wax to save the starch from sticking to the iron.'[12] This last eventuality could also be remedied by rubbing the irons with kerosene as they were taken from the stove, or with soap – 'this is the plan usually adopted by London laundresses'.[13]

When the starch was ready, having been mixed with the chosen additive and diluted with boiling water, the collar, neckband, front and cuffs of the shirts to be treated were dipped and rubbed into it while it was still hot, then left to dry. They were then dipped again into cold starch and rolled up in a thick towel to stay damp. 'When ready, iron all the body of the shirt before touching the starched part. . . . Wring a cloth out of cold water, and carefully rub off the starched surfaces as they are ironed, the particles of starch that lie

Gentleman's shirt (1895)

upon the surface will adhere to the iron otherwise. Collars and cuffs must be rubbed on each side. Use a moderately hot iron, passing it slowly over the surface at first, so that the steam generated by the iron may be absorbed by the ironing sheet beneath; if allowed to come out through the surface, the cloth will blister. When a shirt bosom has been ironed, slightly moisten the surface again with a wet cloth, and iron again, rubbing very hard. This may be repeated indefinitely, each repetition increasing the gloss and stiffness. Collars and cuffs are first ironed on the wrong side, and then finished on the right side.'[14]

An essential piece of equipment for ironing shirts was a special board, known as a bosom-board. It had to be 'made of seasoned wood, a foot wide, one foot and a half long, and one inch thick. This should be covered with two or three thicknesses of flannel, drawn tight and well tacked in place. Cover again with an outside slip of white cotton fitted to the board, and put a clean slip every week.'[15]

After the laborious business of laundering her husband's shirts, it must have been with a sense of relief that the Victorian housewife turned her attention to the other items in his wardrobe. Although the dark colours that prevailed throughout the period did not show up the dirt, they nevertheless became soiled and in need of cleaning. Some woollen cloths could actually be washed; the secret was to use no soap, but instead a pint of ox-gall dissolved in a tub of rainwater. 'When they are thoroughly clean, and all stains are removed, wash them several times in clean water, until the smell of ox-gall is completely removed. They should then be mangled and allowed to remain in the mangle all night, after which they will look new.'[16] If total immersion seemed too hazardous, soiled black coats could be sponged with strong coffee mixed with a few drops of ammonia, or with 'a mixture made by compounding a wineglassful of spirits of turpentine with a teaspoonful of essential oil of lemon. It will freshen up the edges wonderfully.'[17] The lighter-coloured cloths which were used for trousers in the first part of the period and for informal jackets in the second required slightly different treatment; stale bread, fuller's earth or magnesia could be applied to absorb grease, though the latter 'is rather apt to leave a light trace behind',[18] while pipe-clay was considered 'particularly excellent for all grey-coloured cloths. . . . Spread the garment on a clean dresser, and rub the soiled places with a square of prepared pipe-clay, used *dry*. Then pass the clay all over the garment, till quite covered with a white dust. Fold the garment into a compact form, and beat it with some plaited canes till the dust makes its way through from the centre folds. Afterwards shake the material, and brush off the remaining dust with a soft clothes-brush.'[19] Chloroform could be used on the most delicate colours, was very effective and left no smell behind, but 'it requires using with care, and is expensive, sixpennyworth going but a very little way. Still it is a really first-class agent.'[20]

Black cloth does not only become soiled from constant use, it becomes shiny. Various remedies for this were known to the Victorian housewife. The simplest consisted of moistening the shiny parts, and pressing them with a very hot iron over a wet linen cloth. Alternatively they could be sponged with equal parts of hot tea and coffee or rubbed hard with a cloth dipped in a little turpentine. 'Ammonia employed in a weak solution will also have the same effect; but it is not so good, being liable to turn the cloth brown.'[21] A more elaborate fluid could be prepared from 'half a pound of logwood and a few chips of copperas [ferrous sulphate]

Gentleman's waterproof cape (l.) and Chesterfield overcoat (1895)

... boil in three pints of water until reduced to a quart, then add half a wineglass of common gin and a tablespoonful of spirits of wine. It can be applied with a brush, rather a stiff one is best, and when the coat is thoroughly dry brush well with a hard clothes-brush.'[22] But surely the simplest, if also the most surprising remedy is that suggested in the *Tailor and Cutter* in 1879: 'With regard to the question asked by W. L. in No. 602, whether anything would remove the gloss from the back of worsted coats; some few weeks ago one of my workmen offered to remove it from the back of a coat which I had and which was very bad indeed. He succeeded in doing it but would not tell me at first how he did it, but at last he told me he had used urine to rub it with. Whatever it may have been, whether the salt or ammonia contained in it, I know not, but certain it is that the gloss was entirely removed.'

Patent revivers for worn cloth were evidently in use from the beginning of the period, but the results were often lamentable, as Dickens records in *Sketches by Boz*. The narrator has been observing a shabby-genteel man whom he sees every day in the library in an appallingly worn suit. After an absence of a few days, the man reappears: 'He had undergone some strange metamorphosis, and walked up the centre of the room with an air which showed he was fully conscious of the improvement in his appearance. It was very odd. His clothes were a fine, deep, glossy black; and yet they looked like the same suit; nay, there were the very darns with which old acquaintance had made us familiar.... The truth flashed suddenly upon us – they had been "revived". It is a deceitful liquid, that black and blue reviver; we have watched its effects on many a shabby-genteel man. It betrays its victims into a temporary assumption of importance.... It elevates their spirits for a week, only to depress them, if possible, below their original level. It was so in this case; the transient dignity of the unhappy man decreased in exact proportion as the "reviver" wore off. The knees of the unmentionables, and the elbows of the coat, and the seams generally, soon began to get alarmingly white.... There was a week of incessant small rain and mist. At its expiration the "reviver" had entirely vanished, and the shabby-genteel man never afterwards attempted to effect any improvement in his outward appearance.'

Some men's garments required very particular attention. The mackintosh was one of these. Introduced at the very beginning of the period, it was made of Messrs Macintosh and Co.'s Patent

Waterproof Indiarubber cloth, and its problem was that it gave off an unpleasant smell. In 1839 *The Gentleman's Magazine* remarked that 'a mackintosh is now become a troublesome thing in town from the difficulty of their being admitted into an omnibus on account of the offensive stench which they emit,' and in 1880 they were presumably still smelling, since in that year no less than three different devices were patented to prevent this. The resourceful housewife, however, simply wrapped the garment in fresh hay. If it was in need of renovation, the only way was to 'sponge it all over back and front with hot water and then leave it on a dress stand or other figure till dry'.[23]

Scarlet coats were worn throughout the period for hunting, as well as their more obvious use in military uniforms. 'This colour, although very showy, is very easily stained with iron rust, which makes it brown, or with an alkali, which changes it into a dingy crimson. To restore this colour on fine woollen cloth, Mr G. T. Bousefield has secured a patent for the following mixture: Citric acid, 300 grains; carbonate of potash, 150 grains; water, 7500 grains. The citric acid is to be dissolved separately in 4500 grains of water, and the carbonate of potash in 3000. The whole is then mixed together and applied with a sponge. A very dilute solution of the muriate of tin is a better mixture for this purpose than the citric acid and alkaline solution. After being applied and the stain removed, the spot is washed with warm water.'[24]

Although the Victorian housewife was clearly prepared to use chemical compounds on occasion, she must often have preferred to stick to the plain soap-and-water method, which was 'simple, inexpensive, and unaccompanied with any of the risks of injuring the colour incidental to the use of chemicals, and should be always tried before resorting to the more powerful agents which often injure both the colour and fabric of the garment.'[25]

Notes and References

1 Joseph Couts, *A Practical Guide for the Tailor's Cutting-Room, c.* 1843.
2 *The Letters of Jane Welsh Carlyle,* op. cit.
3 *The Gentleman's Magazine of Fashion,* 1849.
4 *The Lady's Newspaper,* 1847.
5 J. C. Flügel, *The Psychology of Clothes,* 1930.
6 Quoted in James Laver, *Dandies,* 1968.
7 Ibid.
8 Reprinted by the *Tailor and Cutter* from a women's magazine.
9 *The Girl's Own Paper,* 1894.
10 *The Queen,* 1870.
11 *Enquire Within,* 1893.
12 *Cassell's Household Guide,* Vol. II, op. cit.
13 Ibid.
14 *Enquire Within,* 1891.
15 Ibid.
16 *Cassell's Household Guide,* Vol. IV, op. cit.
17 *Enquire Within,* 1893.
18 *Tailor and Cutter,* 1889.
19 *Cassell's Household Guide,* Vol. II, op. cit.
20 *Tailor and Cutter,* 1889.
21 Ibid.
22 *Enquire Within,* 1893.
23 Ibid., 1892.
24 *The Ladies' Treasury,* 1875.
25 *Tailor and Cutter,* 1889.

9

Shawls, Bags and Accessories

SHAWLS

Shawls were very fashionable for outdoor wear from the beginning of the period until about 1870, and they continued to be worn by the less fashionable well into the present century.

Their long popularity was based on the fact that they were both simple and versatile. For the less well-to-do, a simple square of checked woven wool was warm, would fit all sizes and shapes, was easy to store, and could alternate as a blanket or a wrapper for the baby. It could also be worn in a variety of ways, depending on the time of day or the occasion. In *Mary Barton* Mrs Gaskell described the Manchester factory girls, for whom the universal outdoor garment was a shawl, 'which at midday, or in fine weather was allowed to be merely a shawl, but towards evening, or if the day were chilly, became a sort of Spanish mantilla or Scotch plaid, and was brought over the head and hung loosely down, or was pinned under the chin in no unpicturesque fashion.'[1]

For the fashionable, a shawl draped round the shoulders and spreading over the wide skirt emphasized the pyramidal shape which dominated Victorian dress until the final disappearance of the crinoline at the end of the 1860s. When made of fine soft fabrics in rich colours, like the much prized Indian shawls, it was a very flattering garment, particularly on the tall and statuesque. When, in *North and South,* Mr Thornton first meets Margaret Hale he is struck by her 'frank dignity' dressed as she is in a simple bonnet,

140

dark silk gown, and 'a large Indian shawl, which hung about her in long heavy folds, and which she wore as an empress wears her drapery.'[2]

The original Indian shawls were made of separate pieces of fine twilled goat's wool, embroidered in bright colours, usually in the cone pattern which has become traditionally associated with them. These were imported into England from the beginning of the nineteenth century and became so fashionable that factories were set up to copy them at Norwich and Paisley. Other materials and techniques were also used, however, and Victorian shawls can be found in almost every possible fabric, including twilled wool, silk, satin, silk and wool gauze, muslin, lace and netting. Shetland shawls, of fine wool knitted in delicate openwork patterns, became particularly popular in the 1840s, and in the same decade imported French cashmere shawls were said to be 'deservedly prized'.[3]

Shawls of muslin, silk, lace and satin would have been cleaned in the same way as other garments made in these fabrics, but the delicate Indian shawls, with their bright embroideries, would probably have been cleaned by a dry-cleaning method such as that recommended by *The Girl's Own Paper* in 1881, for cleaning white woollen shawls: 'Spread a cloth over a table, lay on it the article to be cleaned, powder it well with finely ground starch, fold, powdering at each fold, press well together, cover up for some hours, then rub well together with both hands, shake off the starch thoroughly. If carefully done this process leaves the article as white and fresh as when first manufactured.' *The Queen,* in 1875, recommended a similar method using flour, in which one had to 'rub and wash the shawl in the flour as in soap and water'. The additon of 'a small quantity of powdered blue' would prevent a white shawl looking yellow.

Alternatively, woollen shawls could be washed in a cold, strong, cleaning solution. One version was composed of a pound of soap dissolved to a jelly and mixed with three tablespoons of spirits of turpentine and one of spirits of hartshorn, while another, recommended for cashmeres and merinos, mixed cold soapy water with spirits of wine and purified ox-gall. Coloured shawls were given a final rinse in water containing salt or alum, to set the colours.

Shetland shawls could be washed in a thin lather of soft water and fine curd soap, provided they were handled gently: 'don't rub or wring it, but gently pull it through the fingers'.[4] This method required that the shawls be washed in two separate soap solutions, and then rinsed in water in which there was still a little dissolved soap (enough to give the water a 'milky look') and a teaspoonful of melted loaf sugar, to give it a little body and stiffening.

To ensure that washed shawls kept their shape, they had to be dried very carefully. Many woollen shawls could be mangled, provided that they were first folded between two sheets so that no part of the shawl touched any other part, just in case the colours should run under the force of the rollers. They could then be pressed with a very cool iron. Shetland shawls were simply shaken and then pinned to a sheet spread on the floor by means of strips of old calico tacked to the top of the fringe. The shawl was then left to dry in a current of air.

FANS

Fans were out of fashion at the very beginning of Victoria's reign, but this was only a temporary phase. They began to return to favour in the 1840s and grew in popularity throughout the century. Some were made in England, but most fans were imported from France, China or Japan. They appeared in a variety of materials. Painted vellum or paper leaves, with ivory or mother of pearl sticks, were particularly popular in the 1840s; lace leaves with sticks of bone, wood or ivory, appeared in the 1860s; feather fans were characteristic of the 1870s, and very large fans with leaves of silk, satin or ostrich feathers were typical of the 1880s. After the middle of the 1890s, there was a return to small fans, in a revival of the Empire styles of the beginning of the century. Brisé fans, made entirely of carved or painted sticks of wood, ivory or bone, linked together with ribbons, were used throughout the period, and the firms of Duvelleroy and Rimmel sold plain fans in ivory or enamelled wood, to be painted at home.

Painted fans could not be cleaned, of course, but those made of feathers or lace could be tackled (see Chapters 6 and 7). Plain ivory fans could also be cleaned. According to *The Girl's Own Paper* in 1884, 'To clean ivory fans you might employ more than one method. An American recipe is to rub gently with very fine glass-paper, and polish with finely powdered pumice-stone. But if the ivory be finely carved, so as to preclude such friction, try washing with a weak solution of chloride of lime, taking care not to warp the thin ivory.'

BAGS AND PURSES

During the eighteenth century women had worn hanging pockets under their full skirts, reached through a 'placket hole' in the sides of the skirt and petticoats, so that handbags were unnecessary. With the slim, clinging dresses of the early nineteenth century, however, pockets were too bulky, and bags and purses came into their own. They remained in use even with the wider skirts of the 1830s. As skirts became really full again in the 1840s and 1850s, pockets were temporarily revived, but the smooth line of the cage crinoline ensured that bags were again preferred to pockets, and they remained in fashion for the rest of the period.

Most nineteenth-century bags and purses were made of fabric. Those of the 1830s were often made of the same material as the gown, and worn hung from the belt, but later versions, which could be hung or carried, were made of silk, satin, velvet, plush or fur, and decorated with a whole variety of embroidery techniques

Leather bag for bathing costume, etc. (1873)

practised by the home needlewoman. Many were beaded, and the most popular style of Victorian purse was a long tube of knitted, netted or crocheted silk, often covered with beads and tasselled at the ends, which was slit down the middle and closed by sliding metal rings. Other purses were like miniature bags in embroidered and beaded fabrics. Leather was also used for purses from the beginning of the period, but leather bags were little used until the 1880s.

Fabric bags might be cleaned in the same way as dresses made of the materials, depending on the elaboration of the embroidery and decoration. Leather bags could be cleaned by sponging with a warm, weak solution of oxalic acid. Black leather could be renovated by painting with the following blacking mixture: 'Mix two tablespoons of gin with two of sugar, and thicken it with ivory black. Beat the yolks of four eggs and the whites of two, add to the mixture, and stir all well together. Put on with a brush like ordinary blacking, and leave the articles until dry.'[5]

Parasols and Umbrellas

The Victorians shared none of our adulation of the sun-tan. On the contrary, the Victorian women aimed to achieve a delicate, milky-white complexion, and for this reason the parasol was an essential female accessory.

At the beginning of the period the parasol was small and pretty, covered in plain, printed or figured silk, and often fringed. In the 1850s and 1860s many were covered with lace, and from 1865 they became larger and sturdier in design, with thicker handles. This growth continued into the 'seventies and 'eighties, and typical decorative features included ruched trimming and the use of carved animals and birds on the handles. After 1896, handles became long and elegant, and there was a new fashion for elaborate linings of puffed chiffon.

The style of the parasol also varied according to the place and the occasion. Thus in the late 1860s, *Cassell's Household Guide* recommended plain white holland (a type of linen), gingham or silk for the country or the seaside, but for general walking 'a parasol perfectly plain, or, if the wearer is well dressed, surmounted

Grey silk parasol trimmed with lace (1870)

with a couple of frills of the same material, is in the best taste.'
Separate parasols were used for trips out in the carriage where
their decoration could be displayed to the full, and on these occasions, 'Tussore silk parasols, lined with white or pink are admiss-
able . . . ,' but it was only at fêtes or flower-shows that 'the most
elaborate parasols may be displayed without criticism.'

Parasol fabrics, like umbrellas, could be sponged with the same
cleaning agents used for silk dresses, but the elaborate decoration
on many parasols made them especially difficult to treat. There
were professional dyers and cleaners, and *Cassell's Household
Guide* stated that 'Parasols may be cleaned or dyed for a shilling,'
but clearly, at this time (the late 1860's) this was not always wholly
successful, for the same writer considered that a cleaned or dyed
parasol was suitable only 'for use in the country or for children'.
Amateurs do not appear to have been encouraged to clean their

own parasols, and the only solution for persons 'of good social position and slender means' was to add a black lace cover which made it possible 'to wear for some time a light parasol which is a little soiled'.

Umbrellas were used by both sexes, and were far less decorative than parasols, being much larger and usually covered in some plain dark silk. According to *Cassell's Household Guide*, 'Umbrellas are articles which generally suffer more from careless treatment than from legitimate wear and tear; and an umbrella when properly treated will last twice as long as one that is not so used. When wet, an umbrella should neither be distended to dry, which will strain the ribs and covering, and prevent its ever afterwards folding up neatly, nor at once rolled and tied up, which would tend to rust the frame and rot the textile fabric; neither should it, if of silk, be carelessly thrust into an umbrella-stand, nor allowed to rest against a wall, which would probably discolour, and certainly crease the silk injuriously. It should be shut, but not tied up, and hung from the handle with the point downwards till it is nearly, but not quite dry. It should then be neatly and carefully rolled up and tied. In walking with an umbrella, the hands should be confined to the handle, and not allowed to grasp the silk, otherwise that portion which is held will become greased and discoloured, and the material will be frayed out round the tips, which are points where there is always much stress, and where it will always have a tendency to give way. When not in use, the umbrella should be protected from dust and injury of any kind by its silk or oilcloth case. When dirty, alpaca umbrellas are best cleaned with a clothes' brush; but brushing is useless for those of silk. Ordinary dirt may be removed from a silk umbrella by means of a clean sponge and cold water, or if the soil should be so tenacious that this will not remove it, a piece of linen rag, dipped in spirits of wine or unsweetened gin, will generally effect the desired end. Grease spots should be removed by laying a piece of clean blotting-paper above and below the silk, and passing a hot iron over it.'

METAL LACE AND EMBROIDERY

Metal lace and embroidery was usually reserved for livery, but could also be found on richly decorated items and accessories.

'Gold' lace was in fact composed of lesser metals, presumably with a large element of copper, since there is frequent reference to tarnishing. If the trimming was not too badly tarnished, and could be removed from the garment or accessory, it could be sewn in a clean linen cloth, and boiled in a solution of two ounces of soap in a pint of soft water. After rinsing in cold water it was then pinned out on a cloth to dry. Tarnish could be removed with warm spirits of wine, applied with a soft brush or flannel, but a more drastic method involved removing the trimming and boiling it in slightly diluted hydrochloric acid.

Alternatively, dry cleaning methods could be used. In 1895 *Home Notes* advised rubbing tarnished gold embroidery with finely-powdered rock alum, while *Cassell's Household Guide* recommended the following: 'In an earthen pipkin put some finely-sifted alabaster; put it on the fire to boil, stirring it often with a stick. When sufficiently boiled and well stirred, it becomes very light. Lay the article on a piece of flannel, and strew the powder off with a soft brush.'

Silver lace could be brushed in the same manner with 'calcined hartshorn'.[6]

Notes and References

1   Elizabeth Gaskell, *Mary Barton*, 1848.
2   Elizabeth Gaskell, *North and South*, 1855.
3   *The Lady's Newspaper*, 1847.
4   *The Ladies' Treasury*, 1873.
5   *Home Notes*, 1895.
6   *Cassell's Household Guide*, Vol. II, op. cit.

10

Spots and Stains

'There are few items of more interest to most housekeepers than how to remove spots, take out stains and restore colour to faded fabrics, showing that the staining of their table-linen, spotting of carpets and curtains, mildewing and fruit-staining of the children's clothes is one of the greatest trials to which the busy housewife is subject.'[1]

Nowadays, with so many washable, quick-dry fabrics, the usual response to a bad stain is to wash the whole garment. Considering the time and labour involved in nineteenth-century cleaning methods, however, it is not surprising that the Victorian housewife preferred to find some means of treating only the stain itself. Her approach was cautious and scientific. 'To begin with, before spots or stains can be removed, it is well to know the nature of the stains, as different causes require different treatment. Then, the quality of the goods must be considered. It is very easy to take any kind of a stain out of white cotton or linen goods, while coloured articles must be dealt with more carefully, as most preparations used for erasing stains will injure the colour; then, it is necessary to be much more cautious with silk and woollen goods.'[2]

Here the Victorian housewife had an advantage over her modern counterpart, for not only could she identify the fabric but, in an age when both foodstuffs and household substances such as ink, candles, etc. were produced from known natural products, she could also readily identify the stain.

As recommended, her recipes varied according to the nature of the stain and the nature of the material, but most of them involved the use of bleaches, solvents or acids of some sort. Many were chemicals which are now considered too dangerous for public use, although easily obtained throughout the nineteenth century (see Appendix 2). Other agents were simple products culled from the larder or the garden.

GREASE SPOTS

Then, as now, general grease spots were a frequent problem, and they were usually treated with some sort of spirit to dissolve them. 'Chloroform will take out grease spots, so will salt dissolved in alcohol,'[3] while spirits of wine, naptha or dilute ammonia were also recommended. Alternatively, a combination of heat and absorbent powder could be used, especially on a more delicate fabric like silk. 'Rub French chalk on the wrong side, let it remain a day, split a card, lay the rough side on the spot, and pass a warm iron lightly over it.'[4] Magnesia powder rubbed well in and allowed to dry was said to brush off easily taking the grease spot with it. A more unusual version advised: 'take a visiting card, separate it, and rub the spot with the soft internal part, and it will disappear without taking the gloss off the silk.'[5]

Should the grease have marked a leather glove or shoe, all that was needed was to 'apply the white of an egg to the spot and dry in the sun,'[6] while *Cassell's Household Guide* gave a recipe for all-purpose 'balls for removing grease-stains'. These were made by moistening fuller's earth with lime juice, adding a little pearl-ash, and then making the paste into 'balls about as large as a marble,' which were then dried.

OIL STAINS

'Oil stains on textile fabrics of vegetable origin as cotton, linen, etc., can be removed with solutions of soap and alkalies, whereby the fatty matters contained therein are saponified, and other impurities are then removed mechanically by washing, without materially affecting the colours of the fabrics.'[7] Wool and silk could not be soaped and washed in this manner, however, and for these materials the yolk of an egg could be used as a solvent. Spirits such as spirits of turpentine or sulphuric ether could also be used to dissolve the oil. *Home Notes* claimed that 'strong alcohol, saturated with camphor, has been used with greatest success.'[8] In this latter method the grease was dissolved by the camphor, the alcohol evaporated, and the camphor was then removed by the use of a little water.

CANDLEWAX SPOTS

The widespread use of candles, made from wax, tow or spermaceti (a fatty substance obtained from the sperm whale), was responsible for many grease spots. *Cassell's Household Guide* advised that 'Wax and spermaceti should be scraped off and the places where they have been should be rubbed with spirits of wine, spirits of turpentine, or mephuric ether.'

FOOD AND ALCOHOL STAINS

Food was another major source of spots and stains, particularly beverages such as tea and coffee. Tea was much recommended for invalids, and it was also a fashionable drink for the late evening, when it was served in the drawing-room. Afternoon tea was a fairly late arrival on the social scene, and was probably first introduced by the Duchess of Bedford in the 1840s, but during the latter half of the century it became increasingly fashionable. According to *Home Notes* in 1894, tea stains would yield to the action of 'boiling water poured through them from a height'. Unfortunately, not all fabrics were stout enough to withstand this treatment. *Enquire Within,* in the same year, declared that '"Ignorant" will find it very difficult to get tea stains out of velvet. If I had been so unfortunate, I should try wetting the stains with alcohol. Put a little in a saucer, and rub on lightly with a piece of flannel; then raise the pile by steaming.' Silk, too, required more gentle treatment:

Candles were responsible for many grease spots

'try rubbing the grease spots caused by the milk on a grey silk dress, with a piece of the same silk very perseveringly, of course changing the part of the silk. The friction causes a heat which is analogous to that of a heated iron, but I think myself it is better. I once spilt tea, of which milk was the worst ingredient, on a grey Irish poplin, and the stain quite disappeared by rubbing it in the manner described.'[9]

Coffee was another offender, made worse by the addition of cream. This was the usual breakfast drink, and was also served directly after dinner, the gentlemen partaking in the dining-room and the ladies in the drawing-room. Coffee stains, 'even when there is cream in the coffee, can be removed from the most delicate silk, or woollen fabrics, by brushing the spots with pure glycerine; rinse in luke-warm water, and press on the wrong side with a warm iron. The glycerine absorbs both the colouring matter and the grease.'[10] With a washable material, like cotton or linen, the stain could be treated with a natural emulsion in the form of an egg yolk dissolved in a little tepid water. This dispersed the stain, and when the garment was washed with clean warm water all traces of coffee and milk disappeared.

A popular social alternative to tea or coffee was wine. Wine and biscuits were served to ladies in the middle of the morning, and visitors were often given wine and cake, in the same way that we might provide tea or coffee and cake today. Flora Thompson describes how Laura and her parents paid a morning visit to her well-to-do Aunt Edith, and the little girl was struck by 'a table spread with decanters and wineglasses and dishes of cakes and fruit and biscuits. "What a lovely dinner," Laura whispered to her mother when they happened to be alone in the room for a moment. "That's not dinner. It's refreshments," she whispered back, and Laura thought "refreshments" meant an extra nice dinner provided on such occasions.'[11] Wine was served at dinner, and also at evening functions, where a popular drink was the negus, a glass of port or sherry mixed with hot water, sugar and spices.

If an accident occurred, salt was spread over the wine stain immediately. It absorbed the liquid and was said to be able to neutralize the damage. On linen, 'The salt should be moistened with cold water and left a few days.'[12] Alternatively, 'tie up some cream of tartar in the stained part, and then put the linen into a lather of soap and cold water, and boil about half an hour.'[13] The linen could then be washed as usual and the stain would be completely removed.

Port, with its stronger colour and greater sugar content, was liable to stain more permanently than a lighter wine, and this is perhaps the reason for the rather surprising treatment recommended by *Cassell's Household Guide*: 'If a glass of port wine is spilt on a dress or table-cloth, immediately dash all over it a glass of sherry.' Perhaps the colouring and impurities were diluted by the additional alcohol, and could then be removed more easily, for it was stated that when the stain was rubbed vigorously with dry cloths, no mark would be left. For a lady who had spilt port on her cream serge dress, a more conservative method was to soak the garment in parazone and then wash it.

Enquire Within makes particular mention of 'fruit-staining' as being one of the housewife's greatest problems. Fruit was a favourite dessert, both fresh and cooked. Fresh fruit was often used to form the table centre at evening buffets, where it was piled high on huge platters and epergnes, but it was equally popular for everyday meals. The newly married Cecilia Ridley, in a letter to her mother in 1841, describes a typical dinner in her new home in which there were five courses, the last being 'a sumptuous dessert – grapes, pine [pineapple], brandy cherries, cakes, French plums . . . ,' and she confesses to a particular liking for fruit – 'The grapes I murder are without end. . . .'[14]

According to *Enquire Within*, in 1893, 'Fruit or jam stains can be removed when fresh simply by pouring boiling water through the stain until it disappears. If allowed to remain, fruit stains often become ineradicable. Some recommend rubbing the stains with

A table centre-piece of different fruits

glycerine before pouring the water through, but this is only useful in softening the stain when it has been done for an hour or two.' Apple and pear stains could be removed if the garment was soaked in kerosene for a few hours before washing, for the kerosene acted as a solvent. Where general wetting of the fabric was inadvisable, however, sponging with ammonia was recommended. Alternatively, the stains could be bleached out with sulphur. 'Fruit stains on hands and clothing may be removed by the smoke of a burning sulphur match. Moisten the stained surface and expose it fully to the smoke, which will take effect at once.'[15]

One of the worst fruits for staining is the orange, as it is difficult to cut or eat without spattering drops, and as with all citrus fruits the marks, though invisible when dry, turn yellow with age and heat. Care was always taken when eating these fruits, although few Victorian women would have gone to the lengths described by Mrs Gaskell in *Cranford*. 'When oranges came in, a curious proceeding was gone through. Miss Jenkyns did not like to cut the fruit; for, as she observed, the juice all ran out nobody knew where; sucking (only I think she used some more recondite word) was in fact the only way of enjoying oranges; but then there was the unpleasant association with a ceremony frequently gone through by little babies; and so, after dessert, in orange season, Miss Jenkyns and Miss Matty used to rise up, possess themselves each of an orange in silence, and withdraw to the privacy of their own rooms, to indulge in sucking oranges.'[16] For those who were less careful, and who suffered mishaps, *Enquire Within,* in 1894, recommended rubbing juice stains with the beaten yolk of an egg: 'let it be on for half-an-hour; then wash off with warm water, to which a teaspoonful of liquid ammonia has been added, and press with a warm iron over a bit of old rag.'

INK STAINS

One type of stain which was far more troublesome to the Victorians than it is to us was the ink blot. Their chief writing instruments were dip or fountain pens. Quills were still in use in the first half of the century; they were superseded by steel pens after about 1850, but both types could be messy to use. Hence the numerous patterns for decorative penwipers found in the ladies' magazines of the time. The Victorians also wrote far more letters than we do today for writing was the only means of communication between friends and relatives who were any distance apart. When Cecilia Ridley married and moved away from home, she wrote to her mother almost every day, describing meals, social events, the health of the family, the state of the garden, and discussing politics, clothes, books and mutual friends. She herself admitted that 'My writing case is quite a pet. It gets very thin here with all this good air and hard writing. . . .'[17] Only rarely did the pressure of social engagements, or sickness in the family, prevent her from maintaining her flow of letters, and then only for three or four days at a time. At the end of one such interval she wrote: 'At least I can sit down and write to you a comfortable letter, and really I have been quite distressed at not writing to you for so many days.'[18]

Not surprisingly, ink stains were a frequent occurrence. 'Mr Bowen . . . was a trial to his wife in the matter of "slinging ink". By a particular twist of his wrist when using a pen he could scatter quite a shower of black spots in an infinitesimal space of time. He was also warranted to leave an inkpot wherever it was most in the way, and most invisible to the naked eye.'[19] Many were the ink stains which Mrs Bowen had to tackle. Milk was a favourite solvent for ink. Newly stained linen was soaked in freshly boiled milk for three or four hours. This had the effect of dispersing the stain, which could then be washed out completely with soap and soda. If the stain were already dry, however, it could be boiled up in the milk. On woollen materials, the ink was first dabbed with a cloth, to soak up as much as possible, and then the stain wetted with a cloth soaked in milk. 'Continue gently to wet the spot, then take a clean towel and wipe all over; if well done no stain will remain.'[20]

Another method was to use some sort of spirit or acid. 'Oxalic acid or a solution of salts of lemon will remove either ink or wine stains from any fabric.'[21] Spirits of turpentine were recommended for silk. The stain was soaked in turpentine and allowed to stand for some time; 'then rub it gently between the fingers and the stain will come out, and the colour and texture of the silk be uninjured. This can be done by stretching the silk and putting a drop of the turpentine on it, renewing it until the desired effect is produced. The stain and odour of the turpentine will all disappear in a short time.'[22] According to *Home Notes* in 1894, 'Tomatoes will remove ink and all other stains from white cloth.' This recipe, which relied presumably on the acidity of the tomato, could only have been found in the last decades of the century, for tomatoes were not common in England until the 1880s. Laura caused quite a sensation in Lark Rise when she dared to eat one, and they were considered 'nasty, horrid things' for years afterwards.[23]

The other chief source of ink stains was from the marking ink used to initial underwear and household linen. 'It often happens that in the marking of linen an accident happens, and a blot of ink is made on some exposed part.'[24] Marking ink contained silver nitrate, and the method recommended by *The Queen*, in 1867, was to dissolve it with potassium cyanide ! This was evidently quite easy to obtain from a friendly chemist or photographer, but the writer does add the proviso: 'as it is a deadly poison, the bottle containing the solution should be put out of reach.' *Cassell's Household Guide* advised that 'Two methods may be employed for the purpose of removing the silver by which the mark is caused. The first method is to convert the silver into an iodide, by applying to the stain, spirits of wine, in which iodine has been dissolved. The iodide of silver is then to be removed by means of a solution of the hyposulphite of soda, in which it is soluble. Another method consists in keeping wet the stains with chloride of lime for a few minutes, and then dipping the material in either a solution of the hyposulphite of soda, or in a solution of ammonia.'

MILDEW AND IRONMOULD

Victorian methods of storage were also responsible for stains which we rarely find now, namely mildew and ironmould. (See also Chapter 11). Long-stored and tightly-packed linens were the most susceptible, and the usual methods of removing these fungi involved both cleaning, airing and bleaching the garments. 'Soak in butter-milk and leave on the grass in the sun. Soak several times if necessary, and each time place in the sun to bleach.'[25] Another way is to mix soft soap with powdered starch, with half the quantity of salt, and the juice of a lemon. Lay this mixture on with a brush, and let the linen lay out on the grass for a few frosty nights, and the stains will disappear.'[26]

11 Outdoor dress, 1898. Women copy men with their high collars and tailor-made tweeds. (*The West End Gazette*)

10 Men's day dress, 1886. The light-coloured jacket and matching trousers combine informality with 'order and taste'. (*The London Tailor & Record of Fashion*)

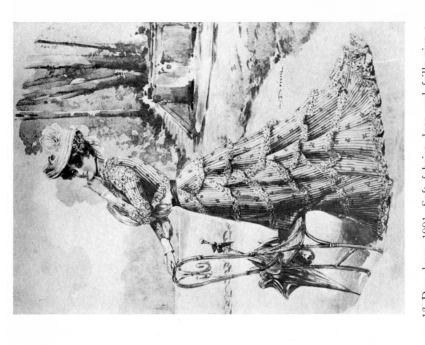

13 Day dress, 1901. Soft fabrics, lace and frills give a gentle, undulating line. (*The Queen*)

12 Outdoor dress of *c.* 1895. Wasp waists are emphasized by huge gigot sleeves.

For dyed materials, which could not be bleached, other methods were recommended. 'Mildewed black lace (as well as black ribbon) can be made like new by steeping it in beer for a few minutes; and after wringing, iron it whilst damp, under a pocket handkerchief.'[27] For coloured fabrics, 'the use of good soap rubbed on the spots, with thorough rinsing and exposure to the sunlight, is probably the safest means.'[28]

Ironmould is a fungus which feeds on the protein in fibres, and particularly on starch, so starched dresses, shirts and frills were particularly vulnerable. Strong acids were needed to remove it. *The Queen*, in 1867, recommended wetting the stain and heating the linen on a plate held over boiling water while at the same time sponging the stain with 'a small quantity of essential salts of lemon' until the mark disappeared. A similar method used half an ounce of tartaric acid and half an ounce of powdered salts of sorrel (i.e. oxalic acid): 'wet the spot with water, dip your finger into the powder, or put a small quantity to the spot, rub it gently, and the ink or ironmould will entirely disappear, without the least damage to the lace, lawn, muslin etc.'[29]

RUST MARKS

Another stain well known in the Victorian age, before the invention of stainless steel, was the rust mark produced by metal fastenings. These marks were removed by acids, in much the same way as ironmould. 'Place the spotted part of the garment over the bowl of hot water. Wet a cork in the muriatic acid, and touch the iron rust with it. Immediately the spot will turn bright yellow. Dip at once in the hot water and the stain will disappear. When all the spots have been removed, rinse the article thoroughly in several waters, and then in ammonia water (a tablespoonful of household ammonia to a quart of water), and finally, in clear water. The acid is very powerful and will destroy the fabric if allowed to remain upon it. Ammonia neutralises it.'[30] (Muriatic acid is a solution of hydrochloric acid, used today to clean down newly-laid brick and tile work. Used in sufficient quantities, it dissolves mortar!)

Alternative methods included spreading lemon juice and salt on the stain and then steaming it; dabbing it with moist cream of tartar and exposing it to the sun; and covering the stain with hot stewed rhubarb. This latter recipe is less surprising when we realize that rhubarb is rich in oxalic acid.

BLOOD STAINS

Blood stains are common to any age, but the Victorian man was particularly prone to shaving cuts from his open razor, and the Victorian woman was liable to accidents from the amount of hand-sewing that she did. Even after the introduction of the sewing machine in the 1860s, much fine work was still done by hand. Thus *Home Notes,* in 1895, commented: 'In sewing upon delicate work sometimes, in spite of the greatest care, a pricked finger will leave behind it a blood stain. This may be removed by the application of damp starch. Put a little ordinary raw starch in a cup, and pour out enough cold water to make it into a paste. With a knife spread the paste upon the stain. When dry shake off, and if a trace of the discolouration still remains, make another application of the starch paste.' Soaking in kerosene was also effective.

SCORCHING

Scorching was another frequent occurrence when it was so difficult to regulate the temperature of one's iron, and when long skirts and open fires were a constant hazard. 'For whitening scorched linen, it is often sufficient to wet it with soapsuds and lay it in the hot sun. Another method is, where milk is plentiful, to put one pound of white soap into a gallon of milk, and boil the scorched article in it.'[31] The favourite recipe, however, involved taking 'the juice of two middle-sized onions, which is boiled in half a pint of vinegar, with one ounce of white soap and two ounces of fuller's earth; the mixture is applied cool to the scorched part, and when dry washed off with clean water.'[32]

MUD, TAR AND GRASS STAINS

Long skirts were also a hazard when walking out of doors, especially on rough ground or in bad weather, but many women preferred to get dirty rather than curtail their outdoor activities. Cecilia Ridley gave the lie to the myth of the demure, frail Victorian maiden when she wrote in 1841: 'I have been riding nearly every day and I have also walked about a great deal in spite of mud. I have some boots that defy all wet and I now feel very bold and independent, and trudge about by myself with great comfort. I make my petticoats very dirty but never mind.'[33]

Petticoats could be washed, but the best way to get mud off a skirt was to let it dry and then give it a good brush. However, *Cassell's Household Guide* did include a recipe for removing mud stains from French merino (a twilled cloth of wool, or wool and silk), which involved wiping the marks with water 'in which a little carbonate of soda has been dissolved,' while *Home Notes* in 1894 stated that mud stains could be removed from black clothes with half a raw potato.

Another outdoor hazard, tar, 'can be easily removed from clothing by immediately rubbing it well with clean lard, and then washing out with warm water and soap.'[34] Grass stains were probably more of a problem, considering the popularity of walking, gardening and picnics. For the latter, *Enquire Within* recommended 'Wetting the spots and rubbing with soap and soda.'[35]

ALL-PURPOSE STAIN REMOVERS

Finally, every housewife had her own recipe for all-purpose stain removers, usually based on some type of solvent, water-softener or spirit, or a combination of these. 'Don't waste the little pieces of soap. Have a good-sized bottle with a big mouth standing in some convenient place and drop them into it. Add ammonia, saltpetre, and warm water, in about the proportion of a tablespoonful of each of the former and a quart of the latter to each pint of the soap, and there will be a mixture excellent for cleaning paint, taking grease from clothing, as well as for many similar purposes.'[36] A cleaning mixture for stains on black cloth or silk could be prepared as follows: 'Rub a handful of fig-leaves into a quart of water, and simmer them down to half. Put the leaves into a cloth, and squeeze out the liquor, which should then be poured into a bottle for use. The liquid should be applied with a soft sponge and gently rubbed until the stains are removed.'[37] This mixture relied on the fact that fig-leaves, like rhubarb, are rich in oxalic acid.

Washable fabrics could be treated by rubbing the stains with the yolk of an egg before washing. Marks on linen could be sponged with salts of lemon, while 'For taking out spots from Black Cloth – Two ounces of powdered ammonia in a pint of rain or soft water. Keep closely corked, as it evaporates. No housekeeper will be without this after once trying it.'[38]

Perhaps the most surprising variant on the use of spirits in cleaning, however, was recommended by *Enquire Within* in 1894: 'Many laundresses wet all spots with whisky before washing the garments.'

Notes and References

1   *Enquire Within*, 1894.
2   Ibid.
3   Ibid.
4   Ibid.
5   *The Queen*, 1863.
6   *Home Notes*, 1894.
7   Ibid.
8   Ibid.
9   *The Queen*, 1868.
10   *Home Notes*, 1894.
11   *Lark Rise to Candleford*, op. cit.
12   *Enquire Within*, 1892.
13   Ibid.
14   *The Letters of Cecilia Ridley*, op. cit.
15   *Home Notes*, 1894.
16   *Cranford*, op. cit.
17   *The Letters of Cecilia Ridley*, op. cit.

18 Ibid.
19 *The Girl's Own Paper,* 1894.
20 *The Queen,* 1868.
21 *Enquire Within,* 1893.
22 Ibid., 1892.
23 *Lark Rise to Candleford,* op. cit.
24 *Sylvia's Home Journal,* 1879.
25 *Enquire Within,* 1894.
26 *The Queen,* 1863.
27 Ibid.
28 *Enquire Within,* 1892.
29 *The Englishwoman's Domestic Magazine,* 1879.
30 *Home Notes,* 1894.
31 *Cassell's Household Guide,* Vol. II, op. cit.
32 Ibid.
33 *The Letters of Cecilia Ridley,* 1841.
34 *Home Notes,* 1895.
35 *Enquire Within,* 1893.
36 Ibid., 1892.
37 *Cassell's Household Guide,* Vol. IV, op. cit.
38 *The Ladies' Treasury,* 1866.

11

Storage

An important aspect of clothes care in Victorian times, and one which is generally disregarded today, was the putting away and storage of clothes.

In these days of small, centrally-heated houses and heated transport, the number of clothes we wear, and the thickness of the materials used, does not vary that much from one season to the next. The Victorians, however, had to contend with lofty rooms, open fires, and draughty carriages, and the only way to keep warm in winter was to pile on layer upon layer of warm clothing. Consequently, it was usual, amongst those classes who could afford sufficient changes of clothes, to have a separate wardrobe for winter and summer, and those items not in use would be put away for several months at a time.

Social conventions also added to the business of putting away clothes, by requiring the Victorian woman to make frequent changes of dress, altering her style according to the occasion or the time of day. Thus, in the middle classes, the lady of the house would don a neat but informal dress for her morning household duties, switch to something more elaborate for afternoon calls, and then change yet again for dinner in the evening. She thus required three basic outfits every day apart from clothing for special pursuits such as riding, walking, parties, balls and visits to the theatre. Lower down the social scale, the housewife who could not afford so many outfits would probably change only her cap during the day, but one, more formal 'best' dress would be brought out on

162

Sundays or for entertaining guests.

Underwear was the other major item for storage, for the Victorian wardrobe included a far greater stock of underwear than is usual today. Every woman had drawers, corsets, chemises, nightgowns and numerous petticoats, to be put away, and since washing and drying took such a time, especially during the winter, it was usual to have extensive sets of each.

Consequently, in a Victorian household, the number of garments in storage at any one time was far greater than is usual today. The care and maintenance of these garments was quite a responsibility, for many problems could arise, particularly with items stored away for any length of time. In Mrs Gaskell's *North and South*, when Margaret, planning to go to a dance, decides to wear her white silk dress, which has been packed away for nearly a year, her mother warns: '"It may have gone yellow, with lying by."' Margaret replies that '"if the worst comes to the worst, I've a very nice pink gauze which Aunt Shaw gave me. . . . That can't have gone yellow."' '"No!"' replies her mother, '"but it may have faded."'

Discoloration from exposure to light and damp, and fading, caused by a combination of light and fugitive dyes, were a frequent source of trouble to the Victorian housewife, but they were not the only problems of long storage. Fabrics left in folds could be permanently creased, and, in the case of stiff materials like silk, this could even produce splitting. Damp, stagnant air could not only turn fabrics yellow, but could lead to the growth of moulds. Such extreme cases were not infrequent, judging by the popularity of recipes for removing mildew. Finally, in an age when all fabrics were either vegetable or animal in origin, all clothing was liable to attack by the clothes moth, furs and woollens being a favourite target. Faced with hazards such as these, it is not surprising that the housewife took great trouble over the location of her storage chests and wardrobes, and the way in which the clothes were put away.

Underwear, nightwear and children's linens could be kept in drawers or shelves in each individual bedroom, but in larger families they might well be stored in a household linen-closet, and appropriate sets handed out to each member of the family at the beginning of the week. Such a closet would have to be large, as it would probably contain both the summer and winter underwear, as well as domestic linens such as sheets, tablecloths and towels. Its placing and organization were thus of prime importance in the running of the household. According to *Cassell's Household Guide,* 'a linen-closet should be contrived against a wall in connection with a chimney where a fire is daily burning.... The gentle warmth which the bricks retain is the best means of preserving linen from mildew, so troublesome to prevent in damp situations.'

It was equally important to check the garments before they were put away. Everything had to be thoroughly clean and dry, for even if the closet itself were free from damp, mildew could soon set in among moist, tightly-packed linens, while any hint of dirt could encourage both mould growth and insect pests. For the same reason, if shirts and petticoats were to be put away for any length of time it was advisable to wash out all the starch first, for starch is a food substance and very popular with moth grubs. Necessary repairs would also be carried out at this time, 'or, if there be not time at the moment to undertake the work, a description of the intended alterations should be written on slips of paper attached to each parcel of goods.'[1]

It was essential to divide the contents of the closet by shelves or parcels in order to avoid confusion, for in an age when virtually all underwear was white and voluminous, and virtually all tablecloths, sheets and towels were white and made of similar materials, one folded article looked just like another. For the same reason, many housewives found it advisable to mark each separate item with the initials of the owner or, in the case of the domestic linen, with the initials of the room to which it belonged. These names were either embroidered or written in marking ink. If marked in ink, according to *Sylvia's Home Journal* in 1878, 'It is far better to mark underlinen in full, and indeed is the general custom now. Were you marking nightdresses, they could be done neatly inside the garment, on the hem where it opens at the front. Children's pinafores can be marked on the hem inside, at the bottom or top. A prettily written name is never unsightly on linen in full view....'

To complete the system, all items put away in the linen-closet were shelved according to type, the shelves labelled, and an inventory of the contents of the whole closet pinned to the inside of the door.

The same principles were followed when putting away dresses, skirts, coats, etc., and considerable attention was paid to their treatment, for, in the words of the *Workwoman's Guide,* 'It is of

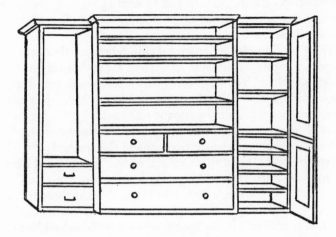

Lady's wardrobe

great consequence that dresses should be carefully and neatly put away, as their preservation depends much on the attention paid to this.'

Firstly, it was necessary to ensure that there was no hint of dampness in the garments to be put away. 'Never put up directly, neither in drawers nor in cupboards, any of the clothes you take off. Open them out, or hang them up in an airy place for at least an hour. Then, after having brushed and folded them, put them by.'[2] All traces of dirt had to be removed. 'Dresses, when taken off, should be well-shaken, and, if silk dusted, if of woollen material, thoroughly brushed. Mantles and jackets the same.'[3] After all, 'Dirt invites moths; and besides, what a satisfaction there is in taking out clothing that is all ready to put on.'[4]

Great care was taken to keep certain types of clothing separate. Winter and summer clothes, for example, were usually kept in separate trunks or closets, not only for convenience, but also to prevent the mixing of different fabrics and colours. 'Care should be taken to separate mourning from coloured dresses, winter clothing from that worn in summer, perfectly white articles from those of a dark colour, as they are liable to be soiled and injured by coming in contact with each other.'[5] In particular, this meant that gentlemen's coats and suits had to be kept apart from their shirts, 'because the darker colour of coats etc., comes off slightly, and would soil the linen.'[6]

When putting clothes away for any length of time, the most important consideration was to protect them from light, which would fade them, and from dust, which would soil and discolour them. For this reason, clothes were rarely put away just as they were, but each individual garment was carefully wrapped up in layers of paper or fabric. The heroines of the short story 'A New-Fashioned Girl' were clearly advocates of this method: '"I wish I had some decent, quiet dress instead of this finery," said Nan, as she drew the once treasured blue silk from its wrap in an old linen table cloth. "I've worn it these two years, straight through, and I am sick of it." "Can't you make a summer dress do?" said the sympathizing Hetty, as she shook her own well-kept white muslin from the blue paper folds her careful mother had placed it in.'[7]

Although blue paper seems to have been the most popular wrapping for white clothing, there was in fact considerable controversy as to the relative merits of different types. *Home Notes*, in 1894, recommended that coats and dresses be wrapped in newspaper and stored in large cardboard boxes. If the newsprint of the 1890s was as prone to smudging as that of the present day, this might well have done more harm than good, and indeed, in 1843, *Miss Leslie's Magazine* had warned readers: 'Never wrap anything in printed paper.' Instead, they were advised that 'All articles connected with dress retain their whiteness or their colour best when put away in coarse brown paper. The chloride of lime used in making white paper has a tendency to turn white articles yellow, and to spot or fade coloured things, particularly silks, satins, laces or ribbons.' *The Workwoman's Guide* also argued in favour of coarse brown paper, on the grounds that 'the turpentine in it excludes the air, and thus preserves the colour more effectually than anything else.' Mrs Tulliver, however, that supreme housewife in George Eliot's *The Mill on the Floss*, wrapped her clothing in silver paper, or in brown holland, a type of unbleached linen. So great was her pride in her clothes care that, even when her visitors were nearly due, she was loath to unpack her Sunday dress until the last possible moment, but wore it 'with a protective apparatus of brown holland, as if she had been a piece of satin furniture in danger of flies'.

Whatever the method used for wrapping the clothes, it was essential that they be properly labelled and listed, or else the owner would soon forget what was contained in each box and bag. For smaller items in particular *Home Notes,* in 1894, recommended storage in stout calico bags, which could be labelled and hung up in a storeroom. 'Imagine the convenience of a row of bags hung up in your storeroom, one labelled children's woollen stockings; another woollen hoods, tippets, gloves, and mittens, and so on. How easy to get them when they are wanted, without diving to the bottom of a miscellaneously filled trunk.'

Folding garments away in bags and boxes was certainly the best means of protecting them from light and dust, but some fabrics could not be treated in this way. Silks and velvets, for example, could be badly damaged if allowed to lie in creases for any length of time, and even the tougher materials could be marked. In 1838, *The Workwoman's Guide* gave long and complicated instructions for folding dresses that were to be put away, so as to avoid too many creases. However, by the late 1860s, when skirts had reached enormous proportions and were beginning to be draped in preparation for the bustle of the 'seventies, even such careful methods were discouraged. *Cassell's Household Guide* declared that 'the elaborate dresses of the present day cannot be folded up and laid in drawers without detriment to their beauty.' Instead, the writer recommended that, before storing away, the skirt be unpicked at the waistband and laid flat. Plain skirts could then be folded, provided that one 'begin at the bottom, and divide the skirt into four equal folds commencing at the middle of the back width; then divide the skirt into cross folds, according to the size desired, taking care to pass the hand between each division to avoid "corner creases".' Presumably more elaborate skirts had their trimmings removed and their draperies unpicked first.

Dresses which had been unpicked, whether because of their elaboration, or because the owner had tired of them and was hoping one day to remake them in a more fashionable style, did not have to be folded, but could avoid creasing altogether if each width of material were wound separately on a roller.

Creasing was not the only way in which fabrics could become badly marked during storage, however, and *Enquire Within* in 1893 was ready to remind its readers that 'Plushes and velvet and the heavier kinds of brocaded silk should be protected from the pressure of the buttons by having tissue-paper put under each button before the garment is laid away for even a week's time.' Considering that at that time it was quite usual to have as many as thirty decorative buttons on a velvet suit, this must have been quite a task.

Even when all these preparations had been carried out, and due consideration given to the dangers of fading, dust and creasing, the careful housewife knew better than to let her clothing lie unchecked for too long a time. Whatever precautions had been taken, damp was a constant threat in the Victorian house, and dresses soon suffered if left untended. In *The Mill on the Floss,* it is obvious to her sisters that Mrs Glegg's silk gown had been in storage 'from certain constellations of small yellow spots on it, and a mouldy odour about it suggestive of a damp clothes-chest.' The only way of avoiding this was to ensure that all clothes were unpacked regularly, taken out of storage, and exposed to the fresh air. Even then, when the time came for them to be worn again, they were not ready for immediate use. 'Some hours before dresses that have been laid aside are worn, they should be shaken well out, and hung before a fire.'[8]

Since most harm to clothing came from long-term storage, the putting away of clothes in daily use caused far fewer problems. Nevertheless, it was not entirely free from difficulty. Today, we take it for granted that while smaller items of clothing and those less liable to crease can be kept on shelves or in chests of drawers, coats, suits and dresses are better hung in wardrobes. This is only the case, however, if they are hung straight, and their weight evenly supported across the shoulders by means of a coat-hanger. Surprisingly enough, this simple and invaluable little article appears to have been virtually unknown to the Victorians, at least before the 1890s.

A type of coat-hanger had already been invented, for at the end of the previous century Sheraton had published a design for a wardrobe with a hanging compartment, in which a brass rail passed through the heads of curved wooden hangers. They could not be removed from the rail, nor could they swivel, but they were certainly a great advance on the wooden pegs which seem to have been common in the earlier part of the eighteenth century. Despite their obvious advantages, they do not appear to have been widely used. Certainly, Gwen Raverat claimed that 'Dress-hangers were unknown in my youth – at any rate to me,' and she grew up in the 1890s.

It was not until 1900 that the author of *Clothes and the Man* recommended his readers to try out the 'shoulders' then used by tailors. According to this gentleman, who used the pseudonym 'The Major', these were 'curved pieces of wood that slip into the collar and project into the shoulders of the coat. In the centre of each wooden 'shoulder' is a stout wire hook, and you hang the coat up by that. . . . These shoulders are quite inexpensive – in fact, a good tailor will give you a shoulder for every coat that you may buy.' Clearly he did not expect his readers to be well acquainted with this device, even at the dawn of the twentieth century.

Without the coat-hanger, then, there were several ways in which the Victorians could hang up their clothes, some of them more efficient than others, judging by contemporary comments. According to the writer of *The Workwoman's Guide,* dresses should be hung up 'either in a closet', although she does not say by what means, 'or on hooks fixed in the wall; they should never be pinned to bed or window curtains, as this very bad practice is apt to tear the chintz.' Thirty years later, 'Sylvia' was equally dogmatic that 'Dresses should not hang too long on a nail. They get into folds that do not look well on the person.'[9]

Despite Sylvia's warning, nails and pegs seem to have been the most usual means of storing dresses in the late nineteenth century, especially among the less affluent. In 1896 *Home Notes* advised occupants of the newly popular bed-sitting rooms that a cheap and simple hanging wardrobe could be made by putting up a row of pegs on the wall and fixing a shelf over them; a pair of curtains could be hung from the shelf to hide the clothes from view. Two years earlier the same magazine had given instructions for fitting a similar curtain to a door, for apparently many flat-dwellers were so short of wall space that the only place available for hanging clothes was on the back of the bedroom door.

Hanging long and heavy coats and dresses from pegs and nails was far from satisfactory, and shelves and drawers seem to have been more popular for the greater part of the period. *The Work-woman's Guide* describes a very convenient wardrobe for ladies' dresses, heavy linen, etc., which consisted almost entirely of shelves and drawers. Admittedly, there was one narrow hanging section for dresses, but they could also be housed on large sliding shelves.

These were probably of the same type as that mentioned in *North and South* when Margaret, remembering how the family had fallen on hard times in her youth, recalls 'The Wardrobe shelf with handles that served as a supper tray on grand occasions.'

Other methods of storage included trunks, boxes or any similar container. *The Workwoman's Guide* recommended that 'For those persons who have not ample space for the number of drawers, etc., requisite to contain their clothes, it is a good plan to have a long narrow ottoman, settee, or sofa, without backs or ends, which is made hollow, and to open; it might be the proper length to stand at the foot of a bed, in a window, etc.'

Men's trousers also provided a storage problem. According to 'The Major', in *Clothes and the Man,* 'the man who has the noble aspiration to keep his trousers in proper shape must begin by having at least seven pairs.' These were only for everyday wear, of course, and did not include those for evening, riding and country wear. Consequently, a Victorian gentleman would have a large number of pairs of trousers to look after and put away. 'The Major' emphasized the importance of taking care of them when they were not in use: 'a pair of trousers that has been properly taken care of will last as long again as a pair that has been "hacked out".' Indeed, it was essential to know exactly how to put them away. 'If you fold the trousers up properly and put them away in a drawer, you have done something for them, but it is possible to go one better than this.' He then recommended a 'trouser-straightener'. This appears to have been a version of the modern skirt- or trouser-hanger, consisting of 'a piece of wood with two other pieces hinged on to it on either side. Each is fastened with a simple clip. Undo one clip, swing back the piece of wood, put your trousers in, bring the piece of wood down again, fasten it with the clip, and your one pair of trousers is in the straightener.' Another pair could then be slotted in on the other side, and the two pairs hung up, 'feet uppermost' by means of a hook attached to the centre piece of wood. To make the best use of these devices, 'The Major' advised that a couple of wardrobe hooks be replaced by two small projecting rods, on which to hang them. 'A rod eighteen inches long will take four trouser straighteners – eight pairs of trousers – comfortably.'

'The Major' also advocated the use of trouser presses, but for short-term renovation rather than for permanent storage.

Smaller items of clothing and accessories were less of a problem to put away; they were usually kept in drawers. A mahogany wardrobe of 1850, said to have been made as a wedding gift for a bride, was fitted in the centre part with twenty-two small drawers with bone or ivory knob handles, and each drawer inscribed as follows:

Satin Slippers	Cuffs
Silks	Habit Skirt
Flowers	Collars
White Lace	Handkerchiefs
Head Dress	Vails
Berthes	Neckerchiefs
Silk Stockings	Bands
Velvets	Ribbons
———	Gloves
———	

Of these, certain items required more care than others. Gloves, for example, were easily soiled, and so, when put away, white, coloured and black gloves were usually kept separate. *The Work-woman's Guide* gives detailed instructions for making a glove case of stout fabric piped with calico, which has separate compartments for the different colours. 'Sylvia', on the other hand, recommends that 'Gloves should not be folded together, but laid flat in a glove box when taken off,' while, according to *Home Notes* in 1895, 'To keep kid gloves soft and in good condition. They should be put in a tin box with a piece of ammonia, which, however, must not touch the gloves.'

Shoes were usually kept in a special compartment at the bottom of the wardrobe, although *Home Notes* in the 1890s is full of hints on how to construct boot and shoe cupboards from old boxes, draped with curtains. Ladies' slippers, intended for indoor wear, were often kept in linen bags, tied up with a draw string. These bags were useful not only in the home but 'to put in one's muff, or to carry in the hand when going out to dine or spend the day.'[10] On such an occasion, the bag could also hold a spare pair of stockings for a ball or party. *Home Notes* particularly recommended that white satin shoes be kept in blue paper, presumably for the same reasons that blue paper was popular for white dresses. They also advised that, if laid by for any length of time, the paper should be covered with wadding to exclude the air and prevent the shoes from turning yellow.

Headgear required more storage space than either gloves or shoes. Ideally, bonnets, hats and the more elaborate caps were kept on turned wooden stands called 'cap poles' in a special compartment of the wardrobe. Alternatively, if there were not enough space in such a compartment, they could be hung on hooks and branches fixed inside the hanging section of the wardrobe. For those flat-dwellers of the 1890s who had few clothes and even less space to keep them in, *Home Notes* in 1894 gave instructions for making a 'combined seat and bonnet box' from a white wood margarine pail, 'which can be procured from any butterman for the small sum of twopence or threepence'. The pail was covered with a suitable material, and the bonnet placed inside on a bonnet stand, secured to the bottom of the pail. If no turned bonnet stand were available, an efficient substitute could be made from a few large cotton reels and a strong iron skewer. Individual hats and caps could also be kept in hat boxes, or wicker cap baskets, although these were more usually kept for transporting the headgear when travelling. Cap baskets, in particular, were most frequently used to carry a special cap to a party or formal occasion.

Bonnet veils were, of course, much easier to store, but even so they could not simply be folded, as the creases would remain in them, particularly if they had got at all damp while being worn. Instead, according to *Home Chat,* 'If a veil is rolled each time after wearing, it will last much longer. A piece of an old broom-handle makes a good roller.'

Clearly, the Victorian housewife was prepared to go to great trouble to protect all her clothes, and those of her family, when they were not in use. One of the greatest enemies in this task, however, and one which would attack all forms of clothing and trimmings made of wool, fur or feathers, was the clothes moth. Today this pest has been vanquished almost entirely by the predominance of artificial fibres, the efficiency of the modern vacuum cleaner and the reduction in the amount of clothing stored away in cupboards and wardrobes. Throughout the Victorian period, however, it was a constant menace.

It is not the moth itself which does the damage, but the grubs. 'The mother moth flies about in search of a suitable place to deposit her eggs, and she selects woollen fabrics or fur, and likes it all the better if it is soiled. The grub once out of the egg feeds on what is nearest it, and so we find an assortment of holes where we left solid cloth.'[11] Furs were particularly vulnerable, as it was difficult to see the moth grubs among the long hairs, and there were numerous methods recommended for keeping furs clean and moth-free (see Chapter 7). Nevertheless, all clothing in storage had to be regularly checked for moth. 'Shut-up cupboards in a house should always be cleaned out every two months or so; and one of the first lessons that the modern housekeeper in a "flat" has to learn is to dismiss her fondly-hoarded rubbish, and only keep about her such things as are in daily use.'[12]

If clothes and linens were kept in a storeroom, *Home Notes* advised covering the windows with fine netting to keep out moths and flies. If moths were suspected, they could be destroyed by placing a lighted candle over a basin of water. The moths would then be attracted by the flame, and, according to the writer, 'will drop into the water.' Alternatively, one could burn camphor to destroy insects, although one had to take care not to cause a fire.

These methods destroyed the moths, but it might be too late if they had already laid their eggs. What was really needed was something to deter them from going near the clothes. *The English-woman's Domestic Magazine,* in 1879, recommended that a rag soaked in turpentine be placed in the clothes drawers for a day. 'Two or three times a year will be quite sufficient. More than this would cause the drawers and their contents to smell unpleasantly.' Other similar deterrents to be kept amongst one's clothes included camphor, pepper, paraffin, cedar wood, Russian leather, and bog myrtle, while to keep moths from furs, *The Queen* recommended 'A piece of tarred rope put into the box with them.'[13] Clearly it was thought that moths disliked anything with a strong smell. One particularly exotic recipe consisted of 'one drachm of oil of cloves, and half a drachm of oil of carraway, to which add a gill of the best gin or whiskey, and also a piece of camphor the size of a filbert; let the whole remain together for twenty-four hours. With this sprinkle the goods, fold them up immediately, and put away.'[14] 'What one's clothes and linens would smell like after exposure to such substances does not bear thinking about. One solution, recommended by *Enquire Within* in 1892, was to scatter them with lumps of stone brimstone. This apparently had the advantage that there was 'no odour perceivable, except by the moths, who very quickly recognise it.' Despite this, it does not seem to have been a very popular remedy, so it cannot have been very effective.

In fact, the very number and variety of the recipes recommended suggest that no real deterrent was ever found, and certainly the efficacy of many was hotly argued. Camphor, one of the most popular, was said by one writer in *Enquire Within*, in 1892, to be positively attractive to moths. 'It is my firm opinion that moths like camphor, and thrive upon it, and that it is a fallacy to suppose that it will kill them or keep them away.' Instead, she advised placing one's woollens and flannels in a box, 'the lid and sides of which have been papered with ordinary newspaper. It is said that moths detest printer's ink, and will not live near it.' Placing candles among one's clothing was an equally unlikely remedy, said to be a 'Certain preventative',[15] while one correspondent quoted the experience of 'the keeper of a large and valuable Government wool and fur store'[16] who thought that moths avoided red woollens, and concluded from this that they must dislike the alum used in their dyeing. According to the writer in *The Girl's Own Paper* of 1898, however, moths had had no scruples in devouring his red plush table-cloth.

It seems, then, that the Victorian housewife had no real solution to the problem of moth, but usually surrounded her clothes and woollens with a barrier of strong-smelling substances, these being the most successful deterrent that she knew.

In many cases she used strong but pleasant perfumes, which served not only to deter moths but also to disguise any hint of mustiness in long-stored clothing. 'A very pleasant perfume, which is also a preventive against moths, may be made of the following ingredients. Take of cloves, carraway seeds, nutmegs, mace, cinnamon and Tonquin beans, each one ounce; then add as much Florentine orris-root as will equal the other ingredients put together. Grind the whole well to powder, and put it in little bags among your clothes etc.'[17]

Perfume bags of dried flowers were also used to sweeten linens and underwear, both women's and men's. When Maggie Tulliver's Aunt Pullet is delving through her stored clothes to find her best bonnet, 'The delicious scent of rose-leaves that issued from the wardrobe made the process of taking out sheet after sheet of silver paper quite pleasant to assist at.'[18] Lavender was another popular choice throughout the period, despite the authors of *The Toilette* who declared in 1854: 'The odour of lavender is, in the present day considered vulgar.' For 'sweet-bags', 'to perfume linen when it leaves the hands of the laundress', they recommended a potpourri composed 'according to the taste of the person using them, of any mixtures of the following articles: flowers, dried and pounded; powdered cloves, mace, nutmeg, and cinnamon; leaves, dried and powdered, of mint, balm, dragonwort, southernwood, ground ivy, laurel, hyssop, sweet marjoram, origanum, rosemary; woods, such as cassia, juniper, rhodium, sandalwood, and rosewood; roots of angelica, zedoay, orris; all the fragrant balsams; ambergris, musk and civet.'

Even dress shoes and gloves could be perfumed. One recipe for gloves involved taking 'Extract of ambergris, four minims; spirits of wine, two ounces.'[19] A cloth was then impregnated with this perfume and used to sponge the inside of the gloves.

When putting her clothes away, the Victorian housewife was as scrupulous in her attention to detail as she was over every other aspect of clothes care. No wonder then, that in the best families taking clothes out of storage was an arduous task. This was certainly the case with the Dodson family, where, on the occasion of a visit from relatives, 'Martha was enjoined to have Mrs. Tulliver's room ready an hour earlier than usual, that the laying-out of the best clothes might not be deferred till the last moment, as was sometimes the case in families of lax views, where the ribbon-strings were never rolled up, where there was little or no wrapping in silver paper, and where the sense that the Sunday clothes could be got at quite easily produced no shock to the mind.'[20]

Notes and References

1 *Cassell's Household Guide,* Vol. IV, op. cit.
2 *The Lady's Dressing-Room,* op. cit.
3 *How To Dress Well on A Shilling A Day,* op. cit.
4 *Home Notes,* 1894.
5 *The Workwoman's Guide,* op. cit.
6 Ibid.
7 *Sylvia's Home Journal,* 1878.
8 *Cassell's Household Guide,* Vol. I, op. cit.

9 *How To Dress Well on A Shilling A Day,* op. cit.
10 *The Workwoman's Guide,* op. cit.
11 *Home Notes,* 1894.
12 *The Girl's Own Paper,* 1887.
13 *The Queen,* 1871.
14 *The Englishwoman's Domestic Magazine,* 1854.
15 *The Queen,* 1870.
16 *Cassell's Household Guide,* Vol. III, op. cit.
17 *Enquire Within,* 1893.
18 George Eliot, *The Mill on the Floss,* 1860.
19 *The Toilette,* op. cit.
20 *The Mill on the Floss,* op. cit.

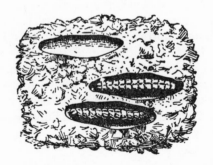

Moth larvae in plush cloth

APPENDIX 1

The Efficacy of Victorian Cleaning Methods and Their Use Today

When faced with the statement that the Victorian housewife spread stewed rhubarb on her underwear, the modern reader may justifiably experience a moment of scepticism. It is a fact, however, that rhubarb stalks and leaves contain a high concentration of oxalic acid. It is also true that oxalic acid is about the best known means of removing iron-mould or rust stains, and is the agent used for this purpose by textile conservators today. Whether the Victorian housewife could have told you that rhubarb contained oxalic acid is another matter; she knew the recipe worked, that is what counts.

Similarly, when one examines the other kitchen or garden products which appear in these recipes, there is generally a sound chemical basis for their use. Vinegar is recommended in a recipe for removing mildew from cottons and linens, because vinegar contains acetic acid, which is noted for its ability to remove certain stains, while at the same time being sufficiently volatile to evaporate before the acid attacks the cellulose fibres of the material. The soapwort plant is recommended as an alternative to soap for washing purposes, and, indeed, it is known to have the same lathering properties as soaps and modern detergents, without the impurities often found in the latter. This product, too, is often used by textile conservators and has recently been rediscovered by many health-food shops as part of the general trend 'back to nature'.

It must also be emphasized that the Victorian housewife knew not only which category of agents to apply, according to the nature of the stain, but which type of agent and technique was most appropriate to the fabric. For example, many silks are damaged by over-wetting, heat and alkalis, while a rubbing or washing action can break the fibres. Consequently, the Victorian housewife chose to sponge on a cleaning solution of alcohol, egg white and sugar, instead of washing in soap and water. The egg white provided a lather similar to soap or detergent lather, and both this and the alcohol would penetrate between the silk fibres, loosening dirt, without actually 'wetting' or penetrating and swelling the fibres themselves. The alcohol would

177

evaporate quickly, and the sugar in the solution would act as an emulsion and would remain to stiffen the fabric.

Similarly, when cleaning gloves, the Victorians knew exactly which process to apply to each type. In the nineteenth century 'kid' gloves were in fact goat or lamb skin which had been treated with minerals such as alum and salt, and the still open pores 'stuffed' with fats, flour and egg yolk to make the skin soft and pliable. The use of water would have removed this stuffing and reduced the leather to a hard, shrivelled state. Consequently, Victorian recipes for cleaning kid gloves relied on dry cleaning methods only. Chamois leathers, on the other hand, were produced by a different process, involving saturation with oils which oxidized into the fibres and produced a supple, durable leather which was washable. For these, therefore, soap and water were readily recommended.

Although, naturally, one variant may have been more successful than another, there is a common logic behind all these recipes. Modern cleaning recipes are based on the same principles, and we have known of great successes using soapwort in washing, absorbent powders to remove grease stains, and stewed rhubarb to remove iron rust. A list of the more popular Victorian cleaning agents, together with a brief explanation of their chemical properties, may be found in Appendix 2.

The Recipes Today

Having given instances of agents that are still valid today, we must add some words of warning as regards the general use of Victorian methods on both modern and historic stains and fabrics.

MODERN FABRICS

All the recipes in this book were intended for use on silk, cotton, linen, or wool. None of them was intended for modern synthetic fabrics and unless the content of a man-made fabric is known, and understood, it is advisable not to stray from the washing instructions supplied by the manufacturer. To give one example: oxalic acid can remove rust stains from cotton or linen, but it can dissolve nylon altogether!

HISTORIC FABRICS

While we hope that we have convinced our readers that Victorian recipes worked for Victorian clothes, we might also add that they were intended for Victorian times. No one ever claimed that they would still be valid for a stain or a fabric that is at least seventy years old. Even supposing that one could identify the soiling or stain after so long a time, the stain itself will almost certainly have undergone chemical changes which make it a very different proposition from when it was fresh. In many cases stains will have formed insoluble matter and will require very specialized treatment.

The fabric, too, may well have altered over the years. One of the major problems facing textile museums is that fabrics deteriorate with age and can become extremely brittle and fragile. Treatments that would have benefited a Victorian fabric when new could well destroy it now. Museums and conservation centres have been working for years to gather information on these chemical changes in order to develop appropriate techniques for cleaning historic fabrics, and the business is far better left in their hands. Your local costume or textile museum will always be ready to give advice.

APPENDIX 2

Victorian Cleaning Agents

Many of the agents used in Victorian recipes, although efficient, were extremely dangerous to use. Sugar of lead and ammonia are poisonous, the acids are corrosive. Benzine and naptha are highly inflammable, and the dangers of using chloroform are obvious. For this reason many items have now been withdrawn from public sale and replaced by modern counterparts that are both efficient and safe. Some of the products can still be found in old-fashioned chemist shops, or through specialist suppliers, but the agents marked with an asterisk in the following list are no longer for general sale in your local chemist shop.

Alcohol: A solvent for fats and oils. Volatile, and thus able to penetrate grease and dirt without over-wetting the fabric.

*Alum: A mineral salt used in treating animal skin, and as a mordant in dyeing.

Ammonia: A strong alkali. A mild bleaching agent and a solvent for grease and paint. Volatile, and so evaporates before the fabric is damaged. Poisonous.

Beer: See *Alcohol.*

Benzine: Obtained from the distillation of petroleum. A solvent for fats and resins. Highly inflammable.

*Benzoin: An aromatic resin from a Javanese tree. Benzoic acid is one of the components of Benzene, a solvent for gums, resins and fats.

Blue-bag or laundry blue: A dye such as ultramarine, indigo, or an aniline dye, added to the rinsing water when washing white fabrics.

Borax: A salt formed from the combination of boracic acid and soda. A grease solvent, water-softener and antiseptic. Toxic.

Camphor: An aromatic substance, probably used as a lubricant. Highly volatile.

Carbonate of potash: An alkali. Potash is a component of some soaps.

Castile soap: Made from olive oil and soda. It dissolves in tepid or even cool water, and is therefore useful for fabrics which cannot withstand hot water.

Castor oil: Obtained from the beans of the Castor oil plant. An excellent conditioner for leather, especially where the leather is polished afterwards.

Chloride of lime: A disinfectant and deodorizer. When mixed with sodium carbonate (washing soda) and water, it produces chlorine bleach.

*Chloroform: An aromatic volatile liquid and grease solvent. An anaesthetic.

*Copperas: Sulphate of iron, also called green vitriol. Used in tanning and dyeing.

*Corrosive sublimate: Mercuric chloride. A strong antiseptic. Protects against mould and insects.

Cream of tartar: Calcium phosphate.

Egg yolk: A lubricant and a medium for other cleaning agents.

Egg white: When beaten to a froth it provides a lather similar to soap or detergent lathers. When dry it forms a stiffening agent.

Fig leaves: Contain oxalic acid.

French chalk: Soapstone or steatite, a soft magnesium powder used by tailors to mark cloth. An absorbent.

Friar's balsam: Tincture of Benzoin (see *Benzoin*).

Fuller's earth: Hydrous silicate of alumina. A fine powder used to absorb grease and other stains.

Gin: see *Alcohol*.

Glycerine: A lubricant for stains.

*Hartshorn: Ammonia. The original source of ammonia was the calcined horns of the hart.

*Hydrochloric acid: A strong acid, useful for the removal of rust and other stains but can damage cellulose fibres. Also called spirits of salt.

Iodine: Used for removing silver stains by converting the silver to an iodide which can be dissolved in sodium thiosulphate. Poisonous.

Isinglass: A form of gelatine obtained from fish.

*Ivory black: A black pigment produced from calcined ivory.

Ivy leaves: Contain oxalic acid.

Kerosene: Obtained from the distillation of paraffin. A solvent for grease.

Lemon: Contains citric acid, a mild bleaching agent.

Logwood: The wood of an American tree from which a black dye is produced.

Magnesia powder: A fine white powder used as an absorbent for grease, etc.

Muriatic acid: Hydrochloric acid and water.

Naptha: Petroleum naptha. A grease solvent and insecticide. Explosive and highly inflammable.

Ochre: An earth containing hydrated oxide of iron which produces a colour range from brown to light yellow. Used as a pigment. An absorbent.

Oil of vitriol: Concentrated sulphuric acid.

Ox-gall: Used in cleaning, painting and pharmacy. Acts in the same way as soap by lowering the surface tension of the water and promoting its penetration into a fabric.

Oxalic acid: The acid of the sorrel family of plants. A bleach and stain-remover, particularly suitable for removing iron rust and ink stains. Highly toxic.

Parazone: Chlorine bleach.

Pearl ash: Potassium carbonate. An alkali.

Pipe-clay: Kaolin, a fine white clay. An absorbent.

Potassium cyanide: Used for removing silver stains. Highly poisonous.

Rhubarb: Contains oxalic acid. The stalks may be used, but the leaves contain a higher concentration.

Rotten-stone: Decomposed silicaceous limestone. Obtainable as a fine powder which can be used as a polish or absorbent.

Sal ammoniac: Ammonium chloride.

Salt: Sodium chloride. An absorbent. Also used for setting dyes.

Salts of lemon: Equal parts of citric acid and cream of tartar.

Salts of sorrel: A form of oxalic acid.

Salts of tartar: Tartaric acid.

Sal volatile: Ammonium carbonate.

Soap bark: the woody part of the soapwort plant.

Soapwort: A plant yielding substances with similar lathering properties to soap. It is usually the dried leaves which are used, but the
woody part can also be utilized (see above).

Soda: A compound of sodium. An alkali. For common washing soda
see *Sodium carbonate*.

Sodium carbonate: Washing soda. A water softener and grease solvent.

*Sodium hyposulphite: A compound of sodium, used for removing
chlorine and iodine stains.

*Spirits of hartshorn: Aqueous solution of ammonia (see *Hartshorn*).

*Spirits of lavender: A mixture of alcohol and ambergris.

*Spirits of salts: Hydrochloric acid.

*Spirits of turpentine: A resinous juice produced from pine and fir
trees. A solvent for various paints, varnishes and waxes.

Spirits of wine: Alcohol.

Starch: Obtained chiefly from corn and potatoes, but also found in
rice and most plants. Used for stiffening fabrics.

Stone brimstone: Sulphur.

*Sugar of lead: Lead acetate.

Sulphur: A bleaching agent. Corrosive.

*Sulphuric ether: A colourless, volatile liquid produced by the action
of sulphuric acid on alcohol.

Turpentine: (see *Spirits of turpentine*).

Vinegar: The sour principle of vinegar is acetic acid. Volatile, and so
evaporates before the acid can attack the fabric. White vinegar is
the purest form.

*Vitriol: Sulphuric acid.

Whiting. A very fine chalk powder. Used as a polish or absorbent.

APPENDIX 3

Items sold in Harrod's Drugs Department in 1895

PART I.
DRUGS AND CHEMICALS.

ACIDS
Acid, Boracic, powder per lb. o/6
   » Acetic per oz. o/1, per lb. o/6
   »   » Glacial oz. o/3, lb. 1/6
   » Carbolic (Disinfecting) per
           bot. o/6½, gal. 4/o, jar o/10
   »   » Pure for Lotions
           per oz. o/4, per lb. 3/6-
   » Citric .. .. » 1/9
   » Muriatic (Spirits of Salts)
           per oz. o/1, per lb. o/6
   » Nitric, Pure per oz. o/2, per lb. 1/o
   » Oxalic .. .. » o/9
   » Tartaric.. .. per lb. 1/3
Aloes, Barbadoes per oz. o/3, per lb. 1/9
   » Socotrine per oz. o/4, per lb. 3/o
Almond Oil .. per bot. o/7½ & 1/o
Alum .. .. per lb. o/1½, o/4
Ammonia, Liquid per 4 oz. bot. o/3
   »   » .. .. per pint o/9
   » Strongest » .. per lb. o/9
   » Carbonate (Lump) » o/9
Antipyrin .. .. per oz. 3/6
   » Effervescing .. » o/9
   » Powders 5 grs. o/10 per doz.
          10 » 1/6 »
          15 » 2/o »
Antimony, Black .. per lb. o/6
   » Butter of .. per lb. 1/o
Areca Nuts .. .. per doz. o/3
   » Nut, Powdered .. per oz o/1½
Aromatic Vinegar .. per bot. o/4
Balsam, Copaibæ per oz. o/3, per lb. 3/o
   » Friar's per bot. o/4, o/7, & 1/2
Benzine, Rectified .. per bot. o/5, o/10
Bicarbonate Potash .. per bot. o/5, o/9
Bichromate of Potash .. per lb. o/8
Bitter Apple or Colocynth powdered » 3/4
   »   »   whole » 2/9
Blue Pill and Black Draught, o/3 doz. 2/6
Borax (Lump) per lb.o/3½, powd. per lb.o/3½
Bromide of Potassium per oz. o/2 per lb.2/6
Calcined Magnesia .. per bot. o/4
Camomile Flowers .. per lb. 1/9
Camphor .. per oz. o/2, per lb. 1/11
   » (Compound Liniment of)
            per bot. o/11
   » (Spirits of) .. » o/10½
   » (Rubini's Essence of) » o/8
   » (Pilules) per bot. o/6 1/o 2/o
   » (Tablets) .. ..each o/2
Camphorated Chalk per box o/2½ & o/5
            per lb. 1/o
   » Chloroform drachm o/2, oz. o/6

Camphorated Oil per bot. o/6 & 1/o
Camphylene .. .. .. per lb. 1/1

CAPSULES—
Ammoniated Quinine 1/6
Blaud's Pills (capsules) 1/2
Cascara Sagrada 1/o
Castor Oil o/9
Cod Liver Oil o/9
Copaiba o/10
Sandal Wood Oil 1/10
Terebine o/10
Carbolic Acid Disinfecting per bot. o/6½
   » » (Pure) per oz. o/4, per lb. 3/6
           Jar o/10, per gal. 4/o
Carbonate of Iron per oz. o/1, per lb. 1/o
 ? » Magnesia (Heavy) per lb. 1/o
   » Soda, Pure » o/4
   » » (Howard's) » o/6
   » » For Household pur-
        poses, /2½ lb. ; 7 lbs. 1/3
   » » bot. with spoon o/9
Carmine per drachm o/6, per oz. 3/9
Cascara Sagrada (Fluid Ext. of)
            per bot. o/10
Castile Soap .. .. per lb. o/6
Castor Oil, per bot. 8 oz. o/6;
       16 oz. o/10½; 32 oz. 1/9
   » (Allen & Hanbury's Taste-
    less) .. per bot. o/5, o/10, & 1/5½
Chalk, Prepared .. .. per lb. o/2
   » Precipitated .. » o/3
   » Camphorated per box o/2½ & o/5
   » (French) Powdered per lb. o/6
Charcoal (Powdered) .. per lb. 1/4
Chemical Food (Parrish's) first quality
     per bot. o/3½, o/6, o/10, & 1/6
Chlorate Potash .. .. per lb. 1/3
Chloric Æther .. .. per bot. o/6
Chloride of Lime .. 1 lb. tin o/4
   » » .. 7 lb. jar 2/2
Chlorodyne (Harrod's) per bot. o/7½,
          1/9, 2/9, & 6/9
Citrate of Iron and Quinine (Howard's)
       per ½ oz. o/4, 1 oz. o/7½
   » » Effervescing, }
         per bot. } 1/5
Citrate of Lithia .. per oz. 1/o
   » of Magnesia, per 4 oz. o/6
       per 8 oz. o/11, 1 lb. 1/6
   » » Extra quality,
       per bot. o/7½, 1/2 & 2/3
Cochineal.. .. per oz. o/3, per lb. 3/o

1070 HARROD'S STORES, Limited, Brompton.
DRUGS.
No. 20 DEPARTMENT—*FIRST FLOOR.*

Cod Liver Oil .. per bot. 0/8, 1/3, 2/4	Gum Dragon or Tragacanth, per lb. 4/0
per gal. 8/6	Hartshorn and Oil .. per bot. 0/5
" " " Harrod's Special Cream	" Spirits of .. per bot. 0/4
Brand, the finest and	Hiera Piera .. .. per oz. 0/3
purest Oil produced	Hops .. .. .. per lb. 2/6
per bot. 1/0, 1/9, & 3/0	Hydrogen Peroxide, extra strong
" " " (Allen & Hanbury's)	per bot. 0/9, 1/6
per bot. 1/1, 2/0, 3/10, & 7/2	Iceland Moss .. .. per lb. 0/8
Confection of Senna per oz. 0/2, per lb. 2/0	Insect Powder .. .. per lb. 2/0
" " Sulphur " 0/1½, " 1/6	" " per tin 0/3½, 0/6½, 1/6, 2/6
Cream of Tartar .. .. per lb. 1/0	Iodine .. .. .. drachm 0/2
Creasote.. .. .. per oz. 0/8	Iodoform .. .. " 0/4
Cubebs (Powdered) .. " 0/4	Ipecacuanha Wine .. per bot. 0/6½
Currie Powder per oz. 0/2, per lb. 2/0	Irish Moss .. .. per lb. 0/10
Cuttle Fish " " 0/2, " 1/0	Iron, Carbonate of per oz. 0/1, per lb. 1/0
Decoction of Sarsparilla per bot. 0/11,	" Dialysed " 0/3, " 2/0
1/9, & 3/3	Jalap, Powdered " 0/3, " 2/0
Dextrine.. .. .. per lb. 0/8	Juniper Berries.. .. per oz. 0/1
Dialysed Iron per oz. 0/3, per lb. 2/0	Kola Nut Powder per oz. 0/3, per lb. 4/0
Dill Seed Water .. per bot. 0/4	Lanoline .. .. per oz. 0/3
Dragon's Blood.. .. per oz. 0/4	Laudanum .. per bot. 0/6 & 1/0
Elder Flower Water .. " 0/5, 0/9	Lead, Sugar of per oz. 0/2, per lb. 1/0
" " Ointment.. per pot 0/4½	Lenitive Electuary or Confection of
Emulsion of Cod Liver Oil per bot. 1/6 & 2/6	Senna . .. .. per pot 0/4½
" " " with Hypo-	Lime Water .. per quart bot. 0/5
phosphites per bot. 1/6 & 2/6	0/1½ allowed for returned
Epsom Salts 4 oz. 0/1, per lb. 0/1½, 0/4	bottle, if clean.
ESSENCES—	" " .. per gal. bot. 1/3
Essence of Bergamot per bot. 0/9	0/7 allowed for returned bottles.
" Cloves .. " 0/5	Linseed, finest English per lb. 0/3,
" Ginger .. " 0/8, 1/3	7 lb. 1/6
" Lemon .. " 0/9	" Crushed per lb. 0/3½, 7 lb. 1/8
" Pennyroyal per bot. 0/6, 1/0	Liquorice Powder (Compound),
" Peppermint " 0/6, 0/10	per bot. 0/4½, 0/8, 1/3
" Senna .. " 0/6 & 1/0	Liquorice (Solazzi) .. per oz. 0/2
Ether, Pure .. .. per bot. 0/8, 1/3	" Root .. " 0/2
" Chloric .. " 0/7	Lobelia .. .. per oz. 0/2
" Spirits of " 0/6, /11	" Dried per oz. 0/3, per lb. 3/0
Eucalyptus Oil .. .. " 0/10½, 1/8	Logwood .. .. " 0/3
Flowers of Sulphur .. per lb. 0/3	**LINIMENTS—**
Fœnugreek .. .. " 0/4	Aconite .. per bot. 0/6 & 1/0
French Chalk (Powder) " 0/6	Belladonna .. " 0/6 & 1/0
Friar's Balsam per bot. 0/4, 0/7, 1/2	Camphor .. " 0/6
Fuller's Earth Powder per box 0/4, 0/7½	" Compound " 0/11
" " " per lb. 0/2	Iodine.. .. " 0/8
Gentian Root .. per oz. 0/2, per lb. 1/0	Soap .. .. " 0/6 & 0/8
Glauber Salts, per oz. 0/1, per lb. 0/1½,	**LOZENGES—**
14 lb. 1/3	Antacid .. per oz. 0/2, per lb. 2/6
Glycerine per bot. 0/5, 0/9, 1/2, qt. 3/0	Bismuth .. per oz. 0/2½, per lb. 3 0
" and Rose Water .. 0/5½, 0/9	Black Currant " 0/2½, per lb. 2/6
" and Tannin .. per bot. 0/6	Cachous (Various kinds), per oz. 0/2½,
Glycerine Suppositories—	per lb. 3/0
Children's size .. per doz. 0/9	Charcoal .. per box 0/10
Adult's " " 1/0	Camphor .. per oz. 0/2½, per lb. 3 0
Goulard Extract .. per oz. 0/3	Cayenne .. " 0/2 " 2/0
" Water per oz. 0/1, per pt. 0/6	Chlorate Potash " 0/2 " 2/2
Gregory's Powder .. per bot. 0/6 & 0/10	Chlorodyne .. per oz. 0/2½ per lb. 3 0
Gum Arabic ,. per lb. 1/3 & 2/6	Cocaine Pastilles .. per box 0 9
" " selected, large per oz. 0/6	Compound Sulphur (Dr. Garrod's),
" Benzoin .. .. " 0/3	per oz. 0/1½, per lb. 1/6

All the above are delivered Carriage Free, subject to the Conditions set
forth on page 4.

HARROD'S STORES, Limited, Brompton. 1071

DRUGS.

No. 20 DEPARTMENT—*FIRST FLOOR.*

LOZENGES (*continued*)—
- Cough Lozenges per box 0/6 and 0/9
- Delectable per oz. 0/2½, per lb. 2/2
- Digestive Tablets per oz. 0/2½ per lb. 2/8
- Eucalyptus Lozs. " 0/2½ " 3/0
- Gelatine .. " 0/1½ " 1/4
- Ginger .. " 0/2 " 2/0
- Glycerine .. " 0/2½ " 2/2
- Guimauve .. " 0/2½ " 2/6
- Ipecacuanha .. " 0/2 " 2/2
- Lavender .. " 0/2 " 2/0
- Liquorice .. " 0/2 " 2/2
- Magnum Bonum " 0/2½ " 2/2
- Marshmallow " 0/2½ " 2/6
- Morphia .. " 0/3 " 3/0
- " and Ipecac. " 0/4 " 3/6
- Paregoric .. " 0/2 " 2/1
- Peppermint .. " 0/2 " 2/0
- " (ext. strong) " 0/2½ " 3/0
- Pontefract Cakes " 0/1½ " 1/6
- Red Gum .. " 0/2½ " 2/4
- Soda and Ginger " 0/2 " 2/2
- Sulphur (Garrod's) per oz. 0/1½ ,, 1/6
- " Tablets .. 12 for 0/6
- Tannin .. " 0/2½ per lb. 2/6
- Tannin, Cayenne and Black Currant, .. per oz. 0/2½ " 3/0
- Tolu .. .. " 0/2 " 2/3
- Voice .. per oz. 0/2½, per lb. 2/2

Magnesia, Heavy Carbonate " 1/0
- ,, Calcined .. per bot. 0/4
- ,, Effervescing Citrate of per bot. 0/6, 0/11, 1/6

Manna .. .. per oz. 0/5, per lb. 6/6
Menthol .. .. each 0/4 and 0/6
Musk .. .. .. per grain 0/5
Nitre .. .. per lb. 0/5

OILS—
- Almond .. per bot. 0/7½ and 1/0
- Aniseed .. .. .. per oz. 0/8
- Bergamot .. .. per bot. 0/9
- Camphor .. per bot., 0/6 and 1/0
- Carbolic .. .. .. per oz. 0/2
- Castor .. per bot. 0/6, 0/10½, 1/9
- Cloves .. .. per bot. 0/6
- Cocoa Nut .. .. .. per lb. 1/0
- Cod Liver, per bot., 0/8, 1/3, 2/4; per gal. 8/6

  Finest Cream Cod Liver Oil, non-freezing and very palatable, specially selected for Harrod's Stores, Limited. Price **1/0, 1/9,** and **3/0** per bottle.
- Eucalyptus .. per bot., 0/10½ and 1/8
- Lavender (English) .. per oz. 5/0
- " (Foreign) .. " 1/0
- Lemon .. .. per bot. 0/9
- Mustard .. .. .. " 0/8
- Olive (extra fine) .. per bot. 1/0

  A rich creamy oil, specially prepared for salads, &c., &c.

OILS—(*continued*)—
- Peppermint (English) .. per oz. 3/6
- " (Foreign) .. " 1/0
- Rosemary .. .. .. per oz. 0/4
- Sandal Wood .. .. " 1/6
- Turpentine (Rectified), per bot. 0/8, 1/0, 1/9

OINTMENTS—
- Bazilicon .. .. per pot 0/5
- Boracic Acid .. " 0/5
- Camphor .. .. " 0/6
- Carbolic Acid .. " 0/5
- Elder Flower .. " 0/4½
- Gall .. .. .. " 0/5
- " and Opium .. " 0/9
- Hamamelis .. " 0/6
- Marshmallow .. " 0/5
- Red Precipitate .. " 0/5
- Precipitate, White .. " 0/5
- Resin .. .. " 0/4½
- Spermaceti .. " 0/6½
- Sulphur .. .. " 0/5
- Zinc .. .. " 0/5

Opodeldoc .. .. per bot. 0/6, 0/8
Orange Flower Water, per bot. 0/5, 0/8, 1/6
Orris Root .. .. .. per lb. 1/4
- " Powdered .. " 1/7

Otto of Roses, per drachm 5/0; tubes 1/10
Oxymel of Squills .. per bot. 0/6
Pepsine .. .. .. per oz. 3/0
Permanganate Potash per bot. 0/4 & 0/6
- " " " lb. 1/3

Peroxide Hydrogen .. .. per oz. 0/2
- " " extra strong, per bot. 0/9, 1/6

PILLS—
- Antibilious .. .. per doz. 0/2½
- Blaud's very superior make, gelatine coated per 100 1/6
- Blue .. .. per doz. 0/2½, 0/5
- " and Black Draught, each 0/3
- Cascara Sagrada .. per 100 1/4
- Cough .. .. per box 0/8
- Liver .. .. .. " 0/6
- Neuralgic .. .. .. " 0/8
- Pennyroyal and Steel .. " 0/6
- Pepsine .. .. .. " 0/5
- Phosphorus .. per bot. 2/3
- " Compound, per bot., 2/3, 4/0
- Podophyllin .. per doz. 0/5
- Quinine, 1 gr., 0/3; 2 gr., 0/4½; 3 gr., per doz. 0/6
- Rhubarb, Compound, .. per doz. 0/2½
- Steel .. .. .. " 0/6

Paregoric Elixir per bot., 0/6 and 0/11
Pepsine Porci .. .. per oz. 3/6
Poppy Heads .. per doz. 0/4
Potash, Bicarbonate, per bot. 0/5 & 0/9

All the above are delivered Carriage Free, subject to the Conditions set forth on page 4.

1072 HARROD'S STORES, Limited, Brompton.

DRUGS.

No. 20 DEPARTMENT—*FIRST FLOOR.*

Pot-Pourri .. per oz., 0/3 ; per lb.   3/6
Pumice Stone Powder   ..   "   0/7
Putty Powder per oz., 0/2 ;   "   1/9
   "   "   0/4 ;   "   4/9
Quassia Chips ..   ..per lb.   0/4
Quinine, per oz., 1/8 ; per ½ oz., 0/11
       ¼ oz., 0/7½ ; ½ oz., 0/4
Quinine and Iron, per oz., 0/7½ ; ½ oz., 0/4
   "   Powders, 1 gr.   per doz. 0/3
   "   "   2 gr.   "   0/4½
   "   "   3 gr.   "   0/6
   "   "   4 gr.   "   0/7
   "   "   5 gr.   "   0/8

Rhubarb Root ..   ..per oz. 0/7½
   "   "   Powdered per bot. 0/7
Rosewater ..   ..   " 0/4½, 0/8
   "   Original   "   0/10
Rouge, Jeweller's, per oz. 0/2 ; per lb. 2/6

Saccharin, Soluble per bot., 0/10, 3/10
   " ;   Tabellæ, 0/7, 1/8, 3/4
Saffron,   per dr., 0/5 ; per oz., 2/4
Sal Volatile, per bot., 0/10 ; per pt. 3/9
Salts of Lemon, per box, 0/3 ; per lb. 2/6
Salts of Tartar   ..   per bot. 0/11
Sarsaparilla, Compound Extract of,
               0/11, 1/9, 3/3
Seidlitz Powders   .. per box, 0/6, 0/9
   "   "   Extra Strong 0/10½
Seltzogene Powders, per box—
   2 pint   3 pint   5 pint
   1/2   1/4   1/9
Senna Leaves   ..   ..per lb. 2/0
Soda, Bicarbonate (Howard's), per lb. 0/6
Spermaceti ..   ..   ..per lb. 2/4
   "   Ointment   per pot 0/6½
Spirits, Camphor ..   per bot. 0/10½
   "   Hartshorn ..   "   0/4
   "   Lavender ..   "   1/0
   "   Nitre   ..   "   0/10½
   "   of Salvolatile   "   0/10
   "   "   "   per pint 3/9
   "   " Turpentine (Rectified),
            per bot., 0/6, 0/10, 1/6
   "   Wine (Medicated), per quart
               bot. 6/4
Starch Powder ..   ..per lb. 0/8
Steel Wine   per bot., 0/6, 0/10, 1/6
Sugar of Milk ..   ..per lb. 1/0
Sulphur, Flower of ..   .. "   0/3
   " . Precip. ..   .. "   0/7
Sulphonal ..   ..   ..per oz. 1/9

SYRUPS—
Buckthorn   ..   per bot. 0/6½
Easton's ..   ..   ..per bot. 1/0
Ginger   ..   ..   .. "   0/4½
Hypophosphites .. per bot. 1/6, 2/9
Lemon   ..   ..   per bot. 0/5½
Parrish's (best quality), per bot.,
            0/6, 0/10, 1/6
Poppies ..   ..   per bot. 0/6
Rhubarb ..   ..   .. "   0/7
Senna ..   ..   .. "   0/7
Squills ..   ..   .. "   0/4
Tolu   ..   ..   .. "   0/5
Violets ..   ..   "   0/6
Tannin   ..   ..   ..per oz. 0/3
Taraxacum, Fluid Extract of per bot. 0/8
Tartaric Acid   ..   ..per lb. 1/3
   "   "   small Crystals for
           Seltzogenes, per lb. 1/3
Terebene (pure)   ..   per bot. 0/8

TINCTURES—.
Arnica ..   .. per bot. 0/3½, 0/10
Bark, Simple ..   "   0/9
   "   Compound   ..   "   0/10
Benzoin, Simple..   "   0/8
Calendula   ..   "   1/0
Cardamoms, Compound "   0/8
Gentian ..   ..   "   0/8
Iodine ..   ..   "   0/6
Lavender ..   ..   "   1/0
Myrrh ..   ..   "   0/6, 0/10
Orange ..   ..   "   0/8
Quinine ..   ..   "   0/11
   "   Ammoniated   "   0/11, 1/10
Rhubarb ..   ..   "   0/10
Senna, Compound   "   0/8
Steel ..   ..   "   0/6
Tonquin Beans ..   .. per oz. 0/9
Turpentine, Rectified
            per bot. 0/6, 0/10, 1/6
Vaseline ..   ..   ..per lb. 1/2
   "   White ..   .. "   1/11
Wax, White   ..   .. "   3/0

WINES—
Ipecacuanha ..   ..per bot. 0/6½
Pepsine ..   ..   .. " 1/6, 2/6
Quinine ..   ..   .. "   1/0
Steel ..   per bot. 0/6, 0/10, 1/6
Zinc Oxide..   ..   .. per oz. 0/2
   " Sulphate ..per oz. 0/1, lb. 0/8

All the above are delivered Carriage Free, subject to the Conditions set
forth on page 4.

SOURCES FOR FURTHER READING

For those interested in the study of Victorian costume, *Victorian Costume and Costume Accessories* by Anne Buck (Herbert Jenkins, London, 1961) is the classic work. The following works are also recommended:

Janet Arnold, *Patterns of Fashion (c. 1660-1860)*, Wace & Co., London, 1964

Janet Arnold, *Patterns of Fashion (c. 1860-1940)*, Wace & Co., London, 1966

C. W. Cunnington, *English Women's Clothing in the Nineteenth Century*, Faber & Faber, London, 1937

C. W. and P. Cunnington, *Handbook of English Costume in the 19th Century*, Faber & Faber, London, 1959

Norah Waugh, *The Cut of Men's Clothes*, Faber & Faber, London, 1964

Norah Waugh, *The Cut of Women's Clothes*, Faber & Faber, London, 1968

To our knowledge, this is the first book on Victorian cleaning methods and clothes care; we cannot therefore refer the interested reader to any other single work. The chief sources for further information on these subjects are contemporary magazines and books on dress. Passing references may also be found in other contemporary writings: novels, letters, diaries, etc. Examples may be found in the notes to each chapter.

INDEX